THE
HEADMASTER'S
PAPERS

THE HEADMASTER'S PAPERS

Richard A. Hawley

BANTAM BOOKS
TORONTO • NEW YORK • LONDON • SYDNEY • AUCKLAND

THE HEADMASTER'S PAPERS

*A Bantam Book / published by arrangement with
Paul S. Eriksson, Publisher*

PRINTING HISTORY

Paul S. Eriksson edition published in 1983

Bantam Windstone Trade edition / November 1984

*Windstone and accompanying logo of a stylized W
are trademarks of Bantam Books, Inc.*

ISBN 0-553-34111-1

Published simultaneously in the United States and Canada

*Bantam Books are published by Bantam Books, Inc. Its trademark,
consisting of the words "Bantam Books" and the portrayal of a
rooster, is Registered in U.S. Patent and Trademark Office and in
other countries. Marca Registrada. Bantam Books, Inc., 666 Fifth
Avenue, New York, New York 10103.*

PRINTED IN THE UNITED STATES OF AMERICA

CW   0 9 8 7 6 5 4 3 2 1

For Tony Jarvis

PART ONE

Mr. Hugh Greeve
Pembroke House
St. Edward's School
Framingham, Massachusetts

Dear Hugh,

I arrived home from the Cape in the dead of night, and it wasn't until this morning that I found your wonderful letter.

Of course you flatter your old—well, seasoned—uncle by deferring so graciously to his years and his experience, as if, in school life, that added up to something reliable. I am not always sure that this is so. Every day of school, at least once, I am aware that what I am doing is completely new, baffling, and that I am empowered with no special skill or insight or strength to deal with it. Remember this admission some time when your own headmaster seems hopelessly pompous or officious. All of us are really, at the nub, timid and desperate—new boys at school, compensating.

But quite frankly, I am flattered that you wrote me. Mainly, however, I am excited about the prospect of your appointment at St. Edward's. For what my opinion is worth, I think the school is just right—small, humane, and standing for something. From what I've been able to see of him, Ted Phillips looks like a promising headmaster to work for. He's so young and earnest he terrifies me. You could do worse than to begin with a young and growing school. But I hope as you become grand and important there you see to it the school doesn't get too big. The limit should be the size at which easy personal acquaintance of everybody in the school is still possible. When a school grows beyond this point, it no longer has a coherent personality, but instead becomes a complex of factions. One experiences big schools as "institutions" and behaves toward them with less than his best intimacy. I think old Endicott Peabody who founded Groton had it right when he said a school should maintain itself as a family (he kept Groton under two hundred boys). But now Groton has gotten bigger than that, and so, I'm afraid, has my shop, although I curse that economically sensible development. A digression—pardon.

Your load is of course overwhelming, but that's as it should be your first year. All of it—the dormitory, the soccer, and the classroom preparation—is essential for getting school life into your bones. This way you will know by the end of a year or two whether School is for you. You will see as the year wears on—often to your horror—that it is futile to try to divide your "inner" personal time from school time. It won't work. The harder you try, the more you will see your (limitless) school duties as an infringement on your "real life." Now everybody feels this strain sometime, to some extent, but my advice is to give in to school life—plunge in and ride the currents, then climb out for refreshment during vacations. (No one has vacations like school people's; we may be broke, but we are granted heavenly stretches of idleness.) The most empty I have ever felt in my schoolmastering days is when I felt I was holding back, saving myself for something. Some day I will tell you about my closet-poet period.

I wish I had some useful insider's tips on starting out, but I'm not sure I do. Something inside is urging me to say "keep out of faculty intrigues," but I know that is impossible. Schools very shortly become close, at times suffocatingly so, but that's part of their value. I think human communities were made to be as intense as school communities actually are. I don't think the culture at large is suffering from too much community but rather from far too little. In schools we do have to live and work with each other intensely. If we are liars, we live through the consequences of our lies. If we are loafers, we experience the reaction of whoever picks up the slack. Everything petty and everything marvelous about each member-soul comes through in a small residential community. The result is often terrifying, and for this reason, especially in the affluent and empty now, the "outside world" often seems a beckoning escape for school people. But you can hardly be interested in escaping, having just volunteered.

Those St. Edward's boys are lucky to be squaring off opposite you. Young faculty are always, in the adolescent mind, bridges to adulthood. Even *dreadful* young teachers, in whose number I would never include you, serve as plausible models of attainable adulthood, while more settled and middle-aged types, no matter how fine or effective, are too remote. Physical youthfulness, apprehension, doubt, impulsiveness—qualities young teachers try so hard to suppress—are wonderfully sympathetic to adolescents. They relate easily to disorder, desperate effort, and posing—these things are, you might say, their life.

How I ramble. What I really have to say is that the prospect of your first year at St. Edward's and your letter to me make me very happy. Although continually humbling, teaching is a wonderful calling. No matter how badly any aspect of it goes, you will never doubt the worthiness of the task. It will always be noble to pass on the best that we know. Perhaps we two might even combine to convince your skeptical father of this before too long. I wonder, really, if my brother didn't throw up those barriers to your taking the St. Ed.'s job just to test your commitment—I wouldn't put it past him. Fathers and sons do seem to have a way of confounding each other, don't they? My own most painful doubts and second guesses revolve around the way I modeled work and adulthood for Brian—apparently quite unattractively. The last we heard he was still living the beach life in Portugal and Spain. Meg and I both pray that he either finds or doesn't find himself soon. We miss him.

Meg of course joins me in sending her love and best wishes. She would add a few lines herself, but she is staying on the Cape to get over some coldy aches and pains and to check out the latest of her wonder doctors in Falmouth. So in the rather dusty solitude of my study, I will now get on to cranking out the thousands of memoranda and agendae which will set our own school year into motion.

I'll have to admit I am looking forward to taking it all on again—all that life!

Love from both of us,

Uncle John

28 August

Mr. Frank Greeve
14 Bingham Drive
Tarrytown, New York

Dear Frank,

Your number one son has paid me the honor of writing me about some of his anticipation about the teaching life. Flattering. What a fine boy, Frank. What a blessing to have his good intelligence, rich experience, and Val's and your good, firm hand behind him as he moves out to take his adult part in the scheme of things.

About our "sharp words" at the cottage—please forgive me. The fault was clearly mine. You were serious and upset about the issue, and I failed to read it. I can see now how flippant I must have seemed. Part of the problem, too, is that I am just so frankly glad Hugh has decided to teach that I failed to pick up your concern. You know, too, I think, that I don't despise "the real world," as you were calling it. I hope I don't need to say that I have always been awed by your drive and your achievement in the firm. More than that, the care and thoughtfulness with which you manage household and personal affairs have always impressed me. And you of all people know I am no enemy to bourgeois comforts. No one would live more pretentiously than I if somebody would only supply the wherewithal. My feeling for your house, household, and manner of living in Tarrytown is one of unabashed envy, not of ascetic superiority.

I suppose what I want to say most is that I hated—was frightened by—the feeling that Hugh's decision was a kind of score in some deep old competition between us. I love school, and I can't help but be glad—for both Hugh and school!—that he is going to try teaching. But that is nothing like a victory for "my side." If Hugh succeeds in the trade—and there is little doubt that he will—it will be, if anything, Val's and your victory. Not to torture an old subject, but I feel anything but victorious in the parenting line. Schoolmasters are supposed to transmit all sorts of wonderful qualities to youth, but you feel just a bit of a fraud when you are having a hard time pulling it off in your own household. I don't mean I've given up on Brian, but I do regret about half the decisions I've made on his behalf. He's still on the Portugal beaches, by the way. In the long haul I wonder what he will make of this vagabond period.

Jenkins arrived promptly and hauled the *Valmar* to the boatyard and with his usual wordless grace said nothing about what would be done, although if he does the bright work again at last year's rates, I'll have to take out yet another mortgage.

Meg's still at the cottage, ostensibly recuperating from a bug, but actually, I am sure, incorporating the last rays of sun into her burnt-umber complexion. For my part, I have forty-eight hours to replace a suddenly resigned math teacher. How deep the vocational commitments of the Now Generation.

Love to Val—
and to you,

J.O.

29 August

Mrs. Margaret Greeve
Little House
Ticonsett Lane
East Sandwich, Massachusetts

Dear Meg,

I called periodically yesterday, but you were out, so I'll write this note in the interest of adding something besides seed catalogs to your waning summer mail.

Arrived late Tuesday p.m. to find the empty house just as bleak and indifferent as I expected. I would like to know what generates dust in a tightly closed-up house. The grounds crew may have cut our lawn once or twice, certainly not recently, and despite our pleas the flower beds have, I am afraid, been ignored. Arnold tells me the crew has been preoccupied with a water-main break under the athletic fields. Whether or not related to this, our tap water is now the color of tea. It's been raining in sheets all day, and there is a pervasive sense of Wuthering Heights about the place—that is, of Wuthering Heights if Heathcliffe had let it to Mr. Chips.

I trust you are well, free of aches, full energy restored. Was that Greek-sounding physician everything you had hoped? Was he expensive—speaking of which: before you close up, could you try a hand at getting some sort of estimate from Jenkins about what his yard costs are going to be for the boat? Frank, being steeped in wealth, doesn't seem to mind paying staggering sums—in fact, seems somehow honored by it, as if they, like yachting itself, were part of being included among the truly established. Anyway, please try with Jenkins. I know I could never do it. One has to admire Jenkins's control.

Rest up. I envy your being there. There is too much going on here for my taste. I finally—and luckily—got a replacement for Frankel in math, a nice woman named Florence something who has gone back to school to awaken her dormant college math major. She is awfully eager and a fast, nervous talker. I hope the boys don't annihilate her. For my part, I am waiting like a crouched panther for Frankel or some future Frankel employer to ask me for a letter of recommendation.

The faculty seem refreshed, and, I'll have to say it, the boys already here for early practices look great. Part of it is normal back-to-school optimism, but part of it is the style of the day. It seems OK now to wear clean clothes, and hair looks less ratty. It is so obvious that the way one turns oneself out bears directly on how one speaks and behaves—how could we have been so dense and so timid over the past ten years? (The curmudgeon raises his scaly head.)

I wish the transition were not so direct, but I am afraid there has been nothing from Brian, here or at school. It's maddening not to be able to get in touch—even to be mad at him, even to send him money! Maybe I am not fully acknowledging my repressed envy of his approach to life. I suppose he has committed himself to systematic truancy as completely as I have committed myself to school. But he is not subtle enough. I too am a little-known part-truant. I too long for the beach. The difference is that I want to play for the other side, too. I crave the release of flight and leisure but, just a little more, I want to know what everybody else is doing and be in on it up to my ears. Which, like it or not, I am. New faculty arrive for "tea" (I have already decided in favor of beer) in half an hour.

Adios, love. Longing to speed to the airport when you give the word.

J.

Mr. Jake Levin
R.D. 3
Petersfield, New Hampshire

Dear Jake,

This is a moment I savor at the end of every summer: a post-midnight hour or so before the business of term really begins: a brown-study's eye of the scholastic hurricane. I actually *am* writing from my, if not brown, at least not very clean, study. All the appropriate mood elements are present—bright moon, crickets, tower bell (electronic, I'm afraid) tolling the hours, even a heightened sense of isolation due to Meg's being away at the Cape another week.

I feel badly about not having written sooner. It's easy to let little fussy business get in the way. I suppose, too, that despite my old-shoe, genial-headmasterly approach to middle life, I let myself be hurt by your no doubt genuine lack of interest in my poetry ms. Odd thing is, I knew when I sent it that you wouldn't like it. Although, despite a few obvious outward trappings, *we* are rather alike, our respective *oeuvres* (yours recognized and official, mine private and skimpy) are irreconcilably different. I know exactly what you mean when you advise me to "pull my oars in" with respect to language, but I don't really know how to do this with my intentions; the "recurring note of adolescent striving" you mention might be less an approach to poems than an approach to life. This would of course explain my vocational destiny as well as my literary limitations.

So how are you? My picture of you up there in the New Hampshire hills is mighty attractive. I'm sure there are lovingly managed near-the-earth routines like hewing wood, stoking fires, and brewing big crude pots of coffee and stew. Seems awfully tempting from my standpoint—especially on the brink of School. I also envy you the time and the quiet to write, to actually get at it. You can actually feel and think freely—and big. By that very fact, though, the writing then has to matter, doesn't it? *It* pretty much has to stand for what you are—which in your case works out happily but which in my (hypothetical) case seems terrifying. Is it nice there? Do you still see/hear from Susanna?

Do you remember you are invited to give another reading and be a classroom guest one day this winter? Expenses of course and all the honorarium I can muster. It will be great to have you here. I don't think Meg's seen you since the last reading. I'll check the date, but I think it's mid-February.

I hope you are well. If I can reconstitute my pride, I'd like to send you some more poems from time to time, as they come up. I would also like to know what you are reading now, at least the nourishing stuff.

I'm off now—must review my opening remarks to the faculty and boys. Right tone must be set, don't you know. Stiff upper lip, most important years of your lives, oldest and most venerable profession in the world (but one) ha ha ha—Christ. Another year like the last will kill me.

I don't think I'll say that.

Best,

J.

3 September

OPENING DAY REMARKS TO THE SCHOOL

To the boys and to the ladies and gentlemen of the faculty and staff of The Wells School—a warm and joyful welcome into our one hundred and sixth year. And to those of you—more than a quarter of you—who are new to Wells this fall, a special welcome. We count on our older boys and staff for continuity, but we rely on our new boys for novelty and vigor.

I suspect there will be plenty of vigor from this new third form, who are ninety strong and who are possibly the most able and most talented class to have been admitted since I have been at the school. Have I said that before? Pardon me. I really do hope that all of you old-timers will extend yourselves a bit and make not only the third form but also the new upper formers feel at home. It shouldn't take much for most of you—perhaps just a brief recollection of how you felt upon arrival here. Let's also give a special welcome aboard to our two new boys from overseas: Helmut Fuerst, our ASSIST student from Cologne, West Germany—will you stand, please, Helmut?—and Paul Conniston from the Westminster School in London. Paul is our English Speaking Union Exchange Scholar. Will you stand please, Paul? Both Helmut and Paul are playing football, or *soccer* as we for some reason call it, and I understand they are doing us no harm. Welcome to Wells, both of you. I hope your year with us is rich and full.

For that matter, I hope this year is rich and full for all of us. I am confident, at least, that it will be full. It always is. Among other things, our board of trustees has charged me to prepare a study to be called "The Wells School: The Next Ten Years and After," to be completed by April first. This report, which will require the efforts of all of us in every area of school life—from studies to athletics, to maintenance, to dorm life, *food,* fuel consumption, the arts—is supposed to be a thorough self-study of what we are now, upon which we can build a viable, healthy Wells for both the short-term and long-term future. If I've made that sound a rather big and vague assignment, that's because it seems that way to me right now. There will be more—I'm sure a great deal more—on that later.

For the most part, we are going to have our hands full with School as Usual, although I'm not sure that school is ever usual. Instead, I'm afraid, School is the opposite of Usual. It's a planned disequilibrium, all obstacles, all challenges. You know a little algebra after last year, so now we'll see if you can know geometry, and if you think you've got that down, trig—and so on. If you thought you were good in third-form English, how about a term paper, a *twenty-page* term paper, with footnotes and a bibliography, an honest bibliography? So you finally moved up the tennis ladder and were playing third singles last spring; how will you fare against the three—or is it four? —nationally ranked new boys? You did all right in introductory French; are you ready to speak it, and nothing else, in class this year? Will you make it into the Group? Will you stay in the Group? Will your roommate work out? Will you be able to face your friends when they come up against you in Student Court? Will the girl you met and liked so much in July remember you when she is back in the lively co-ed company of her local high school or at Middlesex? Are you ever going to reach six feet or five feet eight or five feet six? You are on academic probation; are you going to make it? You are third in your class and captain of everything; are you going to make it? Into Harvard or Duke or Stanford or Williams?

As I said, all challenges and obstacles. But I think it would be a great mistake to try to make school any other way. Except for the challenges and obstacles, how could we find out what sort of persons we are? How would we ever learn which of the prizes are worth having and which don't matter? School—at least Wells School—insists that you *measure up* to things: to mathematics, to composition, to dramatic or musical or athletic challenges, to getting along in an intense, changeable, rather small world of adolescent boys and their teachers. School—at least Wells School—insists that there are worthy things, true things to measure up to. In a way, the school measures you by assigning you this or that grade or by placing you on a first or second team, but more importantly you measure yourselves against past performance, against your more gifted, less gifted, equally gifted fellows, against the system, against the odds.

School can be very intense, and as many of you know, it can make you feel tense, but it also makes you feel alive, sometimes—when you are trying hardest, when you are most engaged—almost *supernaturally* alive. This feeling, rare as it is, is worth pursuing. I think you'll find that it is most likely to occur when you are pursuing or "measuring up to" what is good in its own right: for example, excellence, rather than an 'A' or a victory. Of course real excellence often coincides with 'A's' and victories, but it is a fatal mistake to confuse the two. They are not the same thing.

At any rate, I hope each of you will take on the challenges and obstacles of this school with enthusiasm. Each of you is different and will quite rightly take on school in a different way. But in one important respect you are exactly alike, perfect equals. And in this one respect we will expect the same thing from each of you. I am talking of course about the moral side of things. Besides all those other particular challenges, this school is also going to insist that you measure up to basic honesty and decency. As we have explained to all of you before, new and old boys alike, we are going to insist on your telling the truth and on your treating each other and us teachers as you yourself would like to be treated. These challenges are obvious, ancient, and often very tough. None of us is worth a damn without them. They are not, however, very hard to understand. The quality of this school depends on your meeting them, and so does the maintenance of civilization. There is no way to avoid these challenges, either. They will commence as soon as you leave this hall, if they have not commenced already.

As I was putting these remarks in order last night, it dawned on me with some irony that they were not, really, very original. I'll bet their equivalent were said, certainly more eloquently, by Ionian and Athenian schoolmasters on opening days 2500 years ago. The descendents of those Greek schoolmasters without question told aristocratic Roman boys the same thing five hundred years later when Rome's empire was in the ascendent. And I happen to know that such words were spoken by headmasters Guarino and Vittorino to their Italian pupils fifteen hundred years later still, during the Renaissance. The same things were said, perhaps more forcefully than ever before, by certain great English schoolmasters just over a century ago. So my remarks to you this morning have been terribly unoriginal, but perhaps for that very reason terribly important, too.

The idea that there are eternally worthy and true standards which men can understand and which they ought to measure up to, while very ancient and at times thought to be the very foundation of civilization, is not in style at the moment and has not been in style for a good part of this century. The opposite view—that there are no provable external standards and therefore no obligations to them—takes thousands of forms and is very much among us. If there are no true standards to measure up to, according to this view, the Self is free to do as it pleases. The Self, after all, is supplied with a mixed bag of feelings, some of them marvelously pleasurable, and with standards out of the way, these may be pursued without interference. But, maddeningly, without interference, the pursuit of pleasurable feelings leads to unutterably bad feelings. People get impatient, careless, bored, gross, gouty, alcoholic. They seek remedies from the bottle that caused the sickness. People overdose themselves with liquor or drugs or with sex or with power or with things— even when there is clear evidence that these pursuits are the cause of their dissatisfaction in the first place.

The decade recently passed has been called the "Me Decade," and I certainly hope it is over. I say this not because I am a puritan who hates to see a Self out having a good time, but because of a certainty—maybe my only certainty—that in the long run the Self can't have a good time in pursuit of its own satisfactions. Few of us with the perspective of several decades' time have observed any net increase in energy, productivity, or happiness during the Me Decade. It's been, frankly, a flat and anxious decade. Even the anti-war and ecology sentiments expressed at the beginning have quieted, mainly, I think, because these were movements aimed at measuring up to standards, like justice and world peace and healthy environment. The pursuit of standards and the pursuit of the Self are incompatible.

If we're honest, we admit to feeling driven both ways. If we're honest, most of us will also admit that the selfish drives are stronger; we might *know* better, but it's so easy to do what we feel like doing. Without help, we always do just that.

The help is training. Training. We get it in good families, we get it in enduring religions, and, if we stick to business, we get it in school. It's not always fun, but it really isn't supposed to be. Nevertheless, I think that if you can commit yourselves to business, to "measuring up," you will be surprised, at least if the history of Wells School is anything to go by, at how often fun tends to crop up, often when you least expect it.

Well, I've gotten rather near a sermon, haven't I? But I risked doing it because I wanted so badly to say that I hope you measure up—and that you *want* to measure up—this school year. Incidentally, I hope that I measure up. The fun, I am sure, will look after itself. It always does.

At this point Mr. Upjohn has a few instructions about this morning's meetings, about schedules, and about books. The real business of the day.

Have a very good morning.

4 September

Mrs. Margaret Greeve
Little House
Ticonsett Lane
East Sandwich, Massachusetts

Dear Meg,

Lousy news about the tests. The only thing worse about being in a hospital overnight—even one with a view of Buzzard's Bay—is being in a hospital overnight far from home. I wish I believed that their marvelous instruments could actually isolate the cause of your feeling fluey and run-down. My own dark intuition is that it's the equivocal tap water of Little House. I don't even trust it with toothpaste and have, as you know, come to treat it cautiously with bourbon before swallowing it. But what do I know? You have probably been fighting swine flu, and they have just the thing for it.

I wish my concern for your health were less selfish, but at the heart of the matter, I want you to come back here for my own delight. I want your company. I've grown accustomed to your face. It almost makes the day begin. I want you to cook my breakfast, etc.

My good-hearted colleagues have had me to dinner practically every night, in itself a problem, as each supper is rather a big deal: drinks, fancy things, an enormous roast, more fancy things, etc. I come home bloated and tired and in an unwilling frame of mind to prepare a balanced budget for the Finance Committee of the board. So I write a letter or two, read a bit of something improving, and doze.

The house is very neat, but dusty. The kitchen is spanking clean except for the one tumbler and the one tea cup I use. The lawn is cut, the garden horrendous, but with the falling of the leaves, we can easily conceal them from the public view. I have not had a Faculty Reception yet, because I am afraid that our recent appointment in mathematics, Florence Armbruster or Armature or Armchair, will make a pass at me in my apparent eligibility.

I'll call you Thursday at the hospital, around six. Decide before then what I can send you besides your mail. Write me, love.

J.

P.S. Around noon today, I drove into town to go to the bank, and what should I spy out on the jct. of rte. 9 just past the bridge but a tiny dark-suited hitch hiker wearing a bold, not-yet-spotted Wells tie. Two and a half days and he was headed home for Hartford. He quite naturally assumed I was out on a daily roundup of escaped third formers and dejectedly hauled two mammoth suitcases into the back seat of the wagon. He told me there was no dissuading him. He had "tried it" and it was no good. It seemed to me that there was nothing for it but to go to McDonald's, which turned out to be a stroke of genius, a faint but sure strand of continuity with his hearth and home, such as it must be these days in Hartford. Hardly a scene from *Mr. Chips,* but the lad is staying on. Really a very nice boy, almost garrulous with me now. His name is Marc Slavin, and he is the first in his family to try a private school. Never got to the bank.

5 September

MEMO To Phil Upjohn
Director of Studies

Phil—

Just a note of congratulation and admiration for the way you pulled together opening exercises. Never smoother! Faculty and boy morale seem buoyant. Agree? We ought to keep an eye on Ms. Armbruster though. Seems a little skittish. (I hope young Frankel has been refused welfare and is beating his breast in rage on the West Coast.)

Again, a fine start. We should huddle before the weekend about "Wells Ten Years and After." Ugh.

Best, J.

5 September

Mr. and Mrs. Samuel Slavin
1300 Chafee Circle
West Hartford, Connecticut

Dear Mr. and Mrs. Slavin,

I am writing somewhat impromptu to let you know that I have had the pleasure of making Marc's acquaintance and to share some impressions. He may have told you that his initial experience of Wells was less than rapturous; he tried to go home, but was intercepted. Nothing too unusual in this. Less determined boys just bite their lips

and cry in solitude. At any rate, I think he is going to
stick. One of his roommates shares his interest in lasers
and holography, and he has met another boy in Hallowell
House who is mad about Tolkien.

Incidentally, I find Marc a likable, direct, disarming
person and am awfully glad to have him among us. I hope
you won't hesitate to write or call if you have any concerns about his early progress here.

My good wishes,

John O. Greeve

6 September

Mr. Brian Greeve
General Delivery
Cape St. Vincent
PORTUGAL

Dear Brian,

I am writing to Cape St. Vincent on the slim chance
that you may have returned or that, possibly, you never
left. At any rate, it's the last post office at which we made
definite contact. You know, it's hard to write when you
don't really believe your letter will reach its intended
receiver. For this reason, too, I am enclosing only a
modest money order, but good enough I hope for a few
square meals. If you ever let us know where you are, I'll
be glad to send along a more substantial one. It's not that
I'm getting soft or generous in my old age, only that it's
hard for me to shake the habit of thinking I have an
expensive dependent.

As you can imagine, school has begun, Wells's one hundred and sixth year, and now we are in motion, powerfully,
irrevocably, haphazardly toward June. Hugh has taken a
teaching spot at St. Edward's, a struggling sort of school,
but with a good young head named Ted Phillips. Perhaps
you are in touch with Hugh and know this already.

Your mother has been feeling achey and run-down since

17

the end of the summer and is still on the Cape at Little House. She went into the hospital yesterday for tests, which should drive any flu away. When she gets the results this week, she's coming home. Needless to say, Champ, she'd kill for a word from you. I'd be a liar to deny we worry and wonder about you a great deal. Not that we resent your freedom, but *invisibility*?

Please write.

Much love from both of us,

Pop

10 September

Mr. Frederick Maitland
Headmaster, St. Ives Academy
Derby, Connecticut

Dear Fred,

I am frankly embarrassed to be writing this letter, but too many good people here are upset and too many issues are at stake which would be inappropriate to kick under the Seven Schools rug.

I speak of course about last Saturday's game. I always feel better complaining about games when we have won—when my objections can appear unstained by sour grapes—but this time we were not only beaten but decidedly thrashed. However, that is not the issue.

This is the issue. As I know you were aware, there was really rotten sportsmanship *visible* in that game, almost from the start. What the kids say went on in the line and in pile-ups is perhaps not to be credited, but what we all saw and heard on the field cannot be ignored. Punches and elbows were thrown periodically by both sides throughout the game. Of course that is the officials' business and the officials' fault, but only within their limited sphere. It is also the boys' fault and our fault for letting it go on. I think Jack Kreble did the right thing, although probably not soon enough, in taking out each of our boys he saw fighting, regardless of alleged or observed provocation. I believe he benched four starters on his own. I honestly believe that if you folks had followed suit, we would have gone a long way toward teaching an important principle by example. As it stands, I'm afraid our kids, and maybe some of yours, too, have got the idea that cheap shots work, the way they so often work in big-time televised sports.

The situation wasn't helped, either, by that fellow you had on the P.A. He seemed to confuse the loudspeaker system with a radio broadcast. There was much commentary, hardly disinterested. I bring up this irritating point because amplified praise of one side and derision of the other becomes a factor in play. It was most clearly a factor when your announcer was talking over our signals and over our quarterback's backfield maneuvers. That is simply unacceptable. I have never heard of it in competitive football at any level.

Again, it is embarrassing to have to bring such things up. But doing so might be an occasion for some good teaching. I think it has been here. It's a shame that such a stimulating, gorgeous afternoon became such an ill-tempered and ugly experience for kids, parents, and the rest of us.

Sorry if I'm coming across too righteous or pristine, but I'd feel awfully irresponsible if I didn't share with you what has raised so much passion and concern here since Saturday.

For what my egghead opinion is worth, your football team is three times stronger than ours.

My good wishes,

John

Mr. and Mrs. Loren Engle
125 Sturbridge Road
Chatham, New Jersey

Dear Mr. and Mrs. Engle,

As Roger has already told you, he appeared yesterday before Student Court on a major infraction, his first, and was found guilty. The recommended punishment was return of the records, a written apology to their owner, and that Roger be placed on disciplinary probation for the remainder of the school year.

After meeting with the Faculty Disciplinary Committee this morning, I have decided to accept the court's recommendation, with these reservations and observations. First, I am more concerned with Roger's lack of straightforwardness than with his borrowing—or even pinching—another student's records. Our boys interchange their possessions ceaselessly, usually open-handedly and open-heartedly. That Roger had taken the records without permission and was late returning them would have been routine. What concerns me is that when first asked about the records by their owner, Roger denied having them. When the boy got mad and searched Roger's room, he found them concealed under clothes in a bureau drawer. There were other hesitant and inconsistent admissions in the court sessions as well. As I told Roger just an hour ago, if he had lied to *me* to my face when I asked him about the records, my decision would have been to dismiss him from the school.

Although it could not have been a more cardinal one, this is Roger's first major infraction, and we have no reason to think it won't be his last. By the terms of the probation, however, should he be caught out in another purposeful deception during this school year, we will ask you to withdraw him.

I am sorry to have to convey such unpleasant news so early in this school year. Roger has shown us exceptional aptitude and good personal promise to date, and we have every expectation that this episode represents only a lapse. Please write or call if I can clarify his position further or if you have any other observations or concerns.

My good wishes,

John O. Greeve

12 September

MEMO To Arnold Lieber
Maintenance

Arnold,

What do you mean "nothing" can be done about the Hall before the New Parents' Reception? Of course something can be done. It can be *thoroughly cleaned*. I want that done by tomorrow p.m. if you and I have to do it ourselves.

No more notes, please, about its being impossible to do what we have always done. If you've got a problem with the crew, come see me.

J.O.G.

13 September

Mr. Anthony Rini
1630 Coldport Avenue
Fall River, Massachusetts

Dear Mr. Rini,

I am writing on the outside chance that you might know the whereabouts of my son, Brian. I had word last March that he and your son Leonard had met in Morocco and were traveling together. It is very important that I get in touch with my son, as I have just learned that his mother is very ill. For any information or even suggestions concerning Brian's whereabouts, I will be extremely grateful.

Sincerely,

John O. Greeve

Mr. and Mrs. Robert Taubman
1770 Ashberry Lane
Dedham, Massachusetts

Dear Mr. and Mrs. Taubman,

I am sorry to intrude into your lives again after our last most unpleasant encounter, but a very urgent situation has arisen here which compels me to ask for your help. I have just had word that my wife is seriously ill, and I want very badly to get in touch with Brian. I have no idea if Peggy has had any contact with him, by mail or otherwise, but if she has had, and knows his whereabouts, I would be very grateful if she would let me know. The last contact we made with him was from Cape St. Vincent, Portugal, last spring.

I hope you understand that, in light of the unhappiness you have experienced through Peggy's relationship with Brian, I would not trouble you further for anything but a real crisis, in which I am afraid I find myself.

Faithfully,

John Greeve

13 September

Mr. Jared Thomson
19 Chauncey Street
Cambridge, Massachusetts

Dear Jay,

I am writing on the slim chance that Brian may have been in some sort of touch with you and you might be able to help me locate him. I have just learned that his mother is seriously ill, and I know Brian would want to be aware of that. We last made contact with him in Cape St. Vincent, Portugal, late last spring. If you have even a good guess where he can be reached, I would be deeply grateful.

I hope all is well with you and that a glimpse of light is

possible between immersions in those daunting theological tomes.

My good wishes,

John Greeve

14 September

MEMO To Phil Upjohn
Director of Studies

<u>Personal and Confidential</u>

Phil—

Just a summary of some of the arrangements we discussed last night:

I can see no major problems resulting from my absence, although my two biggest concerns are Saturday's New Parent Reception and kicking off this BLASTED "Wells/future" study. I am confident that you will greet the new parents charmingly. I wouldn't prepare any remarks—just review the third-form program and maybe a few routines (such as discipline, weekends, etc.) You might introduce them to some of the third-form faculty (the presentable ones). Tell them about Dr. Baxter. Whatever comes to mind. It can be very informal. Kitchen knows about punch, etc.

I'm afraid we've got to get organized for the self-study. Bill Truax is already pushing me for data. I suggest we give the boys a half-day next Friday—if we beat Haverhill, make the half-day a prize. Ask the faculty to meet in academic departments and have each department indicate "human" and "capital" needs and priorities in two categories, "immediate" and "long-range"—agree? You and I can then try to make order out of whatever comes in.

I'd like to say I know when I will be returning, but I don't. When we get a green light, we will be in Boston for about a week (?) at Mass. General, then, depending on the treatment program recommended, we will head back here.

Please forgive my being irritatingly repetitious, but it is *very important* that nobody know anything more than that Meg is ill. This is not just so that we can avoid feeling depressed. It may also be an important factor in the course of her treatment. Why not start a rumor that this Boston trip is just a cover to sneak down for some September sun on the Cape? I appreciate your help, and I am sorry to burden further the most overburdened man at Wells.

J.

—Marge has my numbers in Sandwich and in Boston.

14 September

Mr. William G. Truax
President, the Fiduciary Trust Co.
New Haven, Connecticut

Dear Bill,

I am writing to ask if we can delay our end-of-the-month Finance Committee meeting until some later date convenient to you and to the committee. Meg has fallen ill at the Cape and will be checking in to Mass. General in Boston for some tests. I think it's appropriate that I join her. I solemnly pledge not to enjoy myself nor so much as to set sole into a boat. I apologize for the inconvenience but think the situation warrants it.

Preparations are underway for some faculty sessions on "Wells: Ten Years and After," the results of which I will share with you when the full board meets in October.

Please convey my fond regards to Marguerite and to the boys.

Faithfully,

John

Mr. and Mrs. Asa Lewandowski
1446 Trelawney Avenue
Rumson, New Jersey

Dear Mr. and Mrs. Lewandowski,

Thanks so much for your letter, and thanks especially for trusting us enough to tell us about David's condition and medication. I very much appreciate your reluctance to let us know, but it will be a great help to those responsible for him here to know his complete medical history.

It might ease your mind to know that we have had perhaps half a dozen boys here over the past ten years who have been on anti-seizure medication, and each of them has passed successfully through Wells without a hitch. I am sure you are aware that there is considerable evidence to show that an isolated seizure in adolescence by no means indicates an enduring health concern. Medication is often no longer necessary after full growth has been reached.

In keeping with your request, I shall give your letter to Dr. Baxter, our consulting physician, where it will be confidential, and I will tell his swim coach, his dorm master and his current teachers what you have instructed me to tell them.

Please do not hesitate to write or call if you think I may be of any further assistance.

My good wishes,

John O. Greeve

14 September

MEMO To Arnold Lieber
Maintenance

Arnold—

I've been called out of town, possibly for as long as two weeks. It's a bad time, but I've asked Phil Upjohn to

25

assume command. I need your cooperation badly. If he ' asks for something, even for something unusual, *try to do it*. No debates, please. Save your frustration for me when I get back. Help!

J.O.G.

19 September

Mr. and Mrs. Frank Greeve
14 Bingham Drive
Tarrytown, New York

Dear Val and Frank,

It was a great relief and solace to talk to you two last night. Without family, I would literally be lost.

We are now ensconced in our respective Boston settings, Meg in a private room (a term bearing no relation to reality) in Mass. General and I—I'll explain later—at the Copley Plaza. If medical science were less benighted by half, Meg would be at the Copley Plaza and I in the bleak cell. At any rate, Meg is doing beautifully. Her attitude is all shrewdness, attention, and dry humor. Braver than brave—and that is so damned attractive. Dr. Dietrich, the specialist doing the tests and giving the "other opinion," is a thoughtful, likable, humane sort of person—gives the impression of having lots of time and explains things, both to Meg and to me. He won't even venture estimates about treatment, remissions, percentages of cure, etc., until his own tests are in. No false optimism, either. Meg is sick, and it's cancer. I wonder if you can imagine the kind of fear and emptiness that statement arouses in me? I know Meg will endure whatever is required with strength and grace, but I feel like collapsing right now. I keep thinking I've got to *help,* I've got to be strong, but I feel like collapsing. Waiting is worst. I'll keep you posted.

Thank you, Val, for your generous offer to close up Little House and to look after the boat. I left the less equivocal food in the fridge and there is some meat in the freezer you might want to take home with you, if that is technically possible. When you are ready to leave, just call the Frazier number and say, "Come. Close up Little House." He knows what to do about the pipes, and he'll haul the float off to the boat house.

This is all really very strange. Nothing is routine. There is a heavy overlay of irony and foreboding about every practical concern. The *Valmar,* for instance—will Meg and I ever sail in her again? If not, what an odd role that boat has played in our lives: a symbol of possibility, a means to never-quite-worked-out rest and adventure. Our plan was always to sail in and out of quiet Maine harbors, working our way slowly, maybe infinitely, down east. The school would of course give us an autumn leave for this, and we would be happily incognito, out of touch. But as we all well know, such is never the case with boats. The head has always got to be replaced to meet the requirements of the Clean Harbor Commission, the engine is never right, there is always a leak between the engine and the centerboard, unreachable by human hands—not an important leak, just enough to raise the possibility of serious trouble if cruising in cold water anywhere NE of the Cape. But could any actual cruise measure up to our hypothetical one? Probably not. Yard bills buy dreams, not voyages. Or Little House? What does Little House mean without Meg? This is pitiful stuff, I know, but it's the kind of thing I am actually thinking.

Frank, there is one more thing I want to ask which I forgot to mention over the phone. Could you brainstorm a bit with your attorney friends about how I might best locate Brian overseas? I've bombarded the post office at Cape St. Vincent where we last made contact, and I've written to acquaintances he may have been traveling with for a time, but I've heard nothing yet. I think it's very important that he be aware of what is happening with Meg as soon as possible. Are there people-finding services abroad? Do you think our embassies might help? Any tips, hunches, or advice on the matter would be deeply appreciated, Frank.

Again, thanks to both of you. Our best to Hugh.

J.

Mr. Jake Levin
R.D. 3
Petersfield, New Hampshire

Dear Jake,

I am finding this a very hard letter to write because I have something I actually need to tell you. Nothing is easier for me than to make glancing observations; to convey something central is paralyzing.

Meg is ill, very ill. She felt tired, feverish, and achey practically all summer on the Cape, but the symptoms—low grade fever, no appetite, swollen glands, lumps, aches—were somehow so ordinary, except for their duration, that we couldn't bring ourselves to get serious about them. At the end of the summer she had a series of tests at the Cape and then another series here in Boston at Mass. General, and the diagnosis is cancer. It is apparently widespread and relatively virulent, although there have been no visibly dramatic signs of this yet. There are tumors and other irregular growths on her cervix and in surrounding tissue, also in her breast, and probably elsewhere. The cancer has "metastasized."

We have only known something was seriously wrong for a week. The prospect could not be less promising. Neither of us really knows how to respond. It hurts in a new way. It puts you on edge. A weak papery feeling permeates every thought and every activity and fills in the numb spaces in between. The effect is to make everything feel like an anxious *present*. Nothing in the past seems substantial, the future is unthinkable. In this present I keep telling myself the news: cancer. The setting is the off-white, faintly sickly smelling hospital. In spite of the routines and the gadgetry, there is a strange aura of personal unease generated by the staff of Mass. General. I don't think I'm imagining it. A sense of too many people with too much to do. Doctors and nurses seem reticent and haggard. They are reasonable and objective in the manner of my students who are not telling the whole story. Not that they necessarily know the whole story—at least in their heads.

The word for it is cancer, but it is much more than an irregular replication of cells and tissue. At least it's much more than that in a person, in a personality, in Meg. Describing the course of a cancer in terms of what studies show or in terms of treatments, or even in terms of grizzly symptoms and inevitabilities, is not *it*. No more than childbirth is a dilation of the cervix, rapid contractions, expulsion of a fetus and placenta. Like childbirth, cancer is experienced in powerful feelings and a theme. There is pain, depression. For Meg, her "rot," as she calls it, is a summary comment on her adulthood, a consequence in her natural theology she would like to accept, or at least understand. As you know, Meg has always been an expansive, self-effacing kind of thinker. Being sick has made her think about herself and about her body. She will have to consider alternative "therapies"; nauseating radiation vs. nauseating medicines, etc. She will have to decide on terrifying, humiliating surgeries. Such inescapable preoccupation with her physical self is utterly abhorrent to her. The worst thing about the cancer for her is that it trivializes what experience she has left.

Right now we don't know how much time she has. Again, we've only known for certain for about a week. Neither of us has a feeling for cancer's rhythm or velocity. Our most hopeful plan is to get her home as soon as possible, or, if that is not possible, to get her to a comfortable hospital as close to school as we can arrange.

Meg will do fine. Cancer could never diminish her. This morning she said her diagnosis places a damper on some of her plans for a second career. "I had always wanted to start a worldwide mission to save the rich and powerful from themselves."

It is I who may not do fine. Without distraction, I think I could do all right by Meg in her illness. The serving and tending are easy when you love someone thoroughly. What scares me is the rest: school. I haven't let myself think about it, but we're just moving into full swing, and

I can't imagine picking up the reins in a convincing manner. Frankly school—even just teaching school—has always seemed daunting to me. I still have bad dreams about it. But now, since we've been in Boston, it just feels like noise, like a swarming irritable buzz just outside the sphere of what I can, with effort, manage to think about clearly. You can't know what school is like, Jake.

So that's my news. I'm lost.

Write Meg and make her laugh.

Love,

John

26 September

Mr. Frederick Maitland
St. Ives Academy
Derby, Connecticut

Dear Fred,

Pardon me for not responding sooner to your letter, but I have been out of town nearly two weeks and just returned last night.

I must say that I am surprised and disappointed by your response to my letter about our boys' *mutual* conduct at the opening game. Apparently I struck the wrong note and sounded merely wounded and self-righteous. But if that is the case, I failed to represent accurately the feelings and the views of our players, of our coaches, and faculty, including myself. I repeat, Fred, that visible brawling and the audible cursing have no place in a school's athletic program. The problem with its getting out of hand three weeks ago is not that the behaviors occurred in the heat of a battle, but that they seemed to prevail during that battle, as acceptable behaviors, as strategy. This is not a fine point.

Let me be clear about this. I could not care less whether we lost that game, or any game, by a hundred points. We are, as it happens, not very strong this year. But I would like to think that we are all operating from a shared athletic philosophy. And I know that you think so too.

To be honest, Fred, I was bothered by the tone of your response. Even if I *were* guilty of making too much out of too little, I was in earnest in doing so, and I hoped you would respect that.

So, in light of what I have already said, here is my "business." (1) I am writing Dewey Porter, asking him to place on the agenda for the November Seven Schools Conference, a proposed code of uniform athletic conduct—with specific measures to be taken when good conduct is grossly absent. Such a code is probably overdue, anyway. More to the point, (2) I would like to hear from you acknowledging that there *was* unacceptable conduct, on behalf of both teams, in our opening game, and pledging, with me, to take personal action to stop such behavior on the spot should it occur again in contests between our schools. If you do not think you can agree to this request, I am afraid we are not in a position to continue our good competition with St. Ives.

Incidentally, Fred, I *have* considered whether I have "overreacted" to the "rough-housing" in the opener. I do not think I needed the reminder that football is a "contact" sport. The kinds of contact admissible are clearly stated by the rules and by tradition. What both of us observed three weeks ago wasn't boyish high spirits; it was thuggery. Much worse, it was thuggery boosted for a few moments by the support of fans and the lack of appropriate restraints.

We have to do better than this.

Faithfully,

John

Mr. Jared Thomson
19 Chauncey Street
Cambridge, Massachusetts

Dear Jay,

I have just returned from two weeks on the road—in fact, from just across the Charles from you—and so am a little late in thanking you for your kind words and for the efforts you have made to help locate Brian. I have tried to get in touch with the Rini boy myself, through his parents, but have so far had no luck. I shall follow up those other leads, though, and needless to say, will be grateful for any new information you may get hold of. Frustrating!

I will convey to Mrs. G. your warm wishes for a speedy recovery.

What is it that makes a former gypsy turn scholar? Let me know so I can pass it on to Brian.

My good wishes,

John Greeve

27 September

Mr. Samuel Weintraub
Department of Educational Psychology
University of Massachusetts
Amherst, Massachusetts

Dear Mr. Weintraub,

I have been out of town for the past two weeks and have only just now seen your letter proposing Wells School as one of the sites for your study correlating school structures and adolescent values.

I am afraid I must decline on the school's behalf. It is no doubt a sign of my antediluvian education, but I do not happen to believe that real values can be detected by a questionnaire. Adolescents, including our boys, are increasingly savvy about saying the appropriate things, not only on questionnaires but also in forums for free discussion. But the boy who can reason in a clear and sophisticated fashion through a hypothetical moral dilemma in print or in discussion does not necessarily, at least in my experience, behave in a related fashion when confronted with a similar dilemma in his dormitory life. Similarly, the boy who may tick the appropriate columns in the answer forms to indicate that he is tolerant of interracial activity does not necessarily do anything in his daily life to promote it. You would get to know us and our values better by spending a few days here participating in and sharing school life than you would by administering an anonymously taken questionnaire. Moreover, our boys are rather at their limit of standardized tests as it is: D.A.T.s, S.A.T.s, pre-S.A.T.s, Achievements, Advanced Placements, etc.

But while your proposal is not for us, I wish you luck in carrying it out elsewhere.

My good wishes,

John O. Greeve

28 September

Brother Thomas Merriam
Headmaster, The St. Francis Priory
Storrington Rise, Connecticut

Dear Brother Thomas,

Thank you for your letter apprising me of the vandalism done there and of your feeling, no doubt well-founded, that Wells boys were involved. I am appalled by all of it and can relate with special sympathy to the theft of your sign. We have lost dozens since I have been here, and some have been very costly. That yours was so beautifully carved in Carolingian script makes the loss doubly annoying.

The fact that the incident occurred on a *week*night may help us limit our search. We will begin by checking our upper formers' late sign-ins for last Thursday, and I shall begin my own sleuthwork. I suspect whoever pinched your sign wants to have it.

I plan to address the school on the subject and will keep you posted on what follows. Have you thought, too, about Storrington High School boys? My own imperfect intelligence tells me that the passion of their rivalry with St. Francis is unbounded, whereas ours is only borderline pathological.

Let's stay in touch.

Faithfully,

John Greeve

29 September

ANNOUNCEMENT
For Chapel and both lunches
Then to be posted at dormitory landings

It has come to Mr. Greeve's attention that the field house at St. Francis's was spray-painted and their sign removed from its footings last Thursday night, sometime between 10 p.m. and midnight. There is good reason to think that Wells boys were involved. The missing sign is one of a kind, valuable, and an important tradition of St. Francis Priory.

If any Wells boys were involved in this vandalism, they are invited to make themselves known to Mr. Greeve today or tomorrow. Whoever does so will be placed on disciplinary probation for the rest of the term, will be responsible for cleaning the fieldhouse, and will be required to return or to replace the sign. If Mr. Greeve, through his own efforts, identifies a Wells boy or boys as the offenders, that boy or those boys will be dismissed from the school.

Mr. and Mrs. Frank Greeve
14 Bingham Drive
Tarrytown, New York

Dear Val and Frank,

Sorry for the tardy correspondence, but school has been proceeding just as if my life were not in disarray. It is my mature feeling as a schoolmaster that over the centuries during which schools have been established to pass on the culture to adolescents, the cumulative gains have been exactly zero. Every single boy seems to have to try being a laggard, thief, cheat, lunatic, solitary, etc., for himself. That you and I and millions of others have already learned these lessons matters not at all to these hell-bent *tabulae rasae*. This evening as I was walking from my tidy school study to my untidy home study, a dorm master presented me with a badly shaken third former who had escalated some dorm room rivalry by urinating copiously into a balloon and then chucking this dreadful missile through the open door of his enemies. Are there appropriate words of rebuke for such an infraction? What, if anything, shall I write the parents without their losing all hope? The boy won my heart, though, by offering absolutely nothing in his own defense. Sometimes I think of my Prize Day speeches or Addresses to New Parents about the beautiful mission of youth and about my own beautiful mission *to* youth, and then I think of things like flying balloons full of urine.

The plant and the books are greatly appreciated by Meg. She is for the moment reasonably comfortable at the clinic. She has made the decision to have no surgeries, and this has been awfully hard for her. I agree with her completely, although the decision carries with it the certainty that she will have less time and probably more pain, sooner. One thing we had not thought of was that given the nature of this particular kind of cancer and of its medications, she has virtually no immunity or resistance to anything else. Among other things, this means that the possibility of homestays, even on a temporary basis, is doubtful. This hurts, as it's the thing Meg wanted most. She says she can't imagine being scared of anything at home in her own bed. We shall have to see. For the time being, she seems to be managing well. She has little interest in food, but she reads voraciously between jabs and intrusions from the nurses, and her conversation is still in top form. She asks after you without cease. For my sake, too, I hope your projected New England run works out. It would be good for you to see her while she is still relatively strong.

Thanks, Frank, for helping me wrestle with the Brian problem. It's maddening when there is no promising starting point. I have no idea what country he's in—or even what continent. I find this makes me so irrationally angry at him I can't sleep. Then I begin torturously to imagine all the sad and vile things—including the worst—that might have happened to him. Nevertheless, if he should cruise in casually six months hence all hairy and rumpled with another incomprehensible companion in tow and learn that his mother is dead, that would be a guilt and a sadness I would like very much to lighten. We shall see.

I think I'm glad school keeps me preoccupied. It's quite different this year: running very powerfully down wind with a wobbly, undersized tiller and no other point of sail possible.

Hope to see you soon.

Love, John

1 October

Separate copies to
  the parents of:
Toby Witherington (6th)
Tom Foster (6th)
Charles DeMas (5th)

Dear Mr. and Mrs. ——————

By now —————— has possibly told you that he has, along with two companions, been placed on disciplin-

36

ary probation for the remainder of the term for a Major Infraction: spray-painting a wall of the St. Francis Priory field house and removing and concealing the school sign. This foray behind St. Francis's lines also entailed signing out falsely, thereby violating the school's honor code—an infraction every bit as serious as the vandalism.

"Vandalism" may sound harsh, but I am going to retain the term. What the boys had in mind, frankly, was something of a lark. And that, in our opinion, was what it mainly was, although I don't think I'll tell them that. For your information, no harm was finally done. The boys will experience the decidedly appropriate humiliation of two long weekend afternoons scouring and repainting a large fieldhouse wall, and they have already returned undamaged the sign from its place of concealment.

You can be proud of the forthright manner in which they confessed—albeit under a fairly stern ultimatum from me. They are good boys who have each put together a creditable record of achievement and service here. Please be assured that this stunt, provided its like does not recur too often, will do nothing to mar that record.

I hope you will not hesitate to write or call if I can be of any further assistance or if I can clarify——————'s disciplinary status at the school.

My good wishes,

John O. Greeve

1 October

Brother Thomas Merriam
Headmaster, St. Francis Priory
Storrington Rise, Connecticut

Dear Brother Thomas,

Thanks very much for your warm note. I'm glad you had a chance to meet the boys, and that your facilities will be restored to order by next weekend. Justice done, I think.

Yes, they are good boys—but maybe not that good. They

have received a just penance and an opportunity to confront the likes of you, which they will always, with a little trepidation, remember. I don't know whether to say they had their cake and ate it too, or that they had two cakes and ate neither of them. I'm sure you will see what I mean.

Anyway, thank you for not being so regardful or timid or busy as to let the thing drop. You have given three promising rascals an important experience.

For your information, we've wired up our own sign to lethal voltage. Pass the word around.

Faithfully,

John Greeve

3 October

Mr. Jake Levin
R.D. 3
Petersfield, New Hampshire

Dear Jake,

Thanks very much for *A Grief Observed.* I have very mixed feelings about it. First, that you, staunchest of pagans (or so I had always been led to believe), should send me a reflection by a popular Christian apologist is a phenomenon worth thinking about. I read the book straight off, but if I hadn't I would have wondered what you had in mind sending me Lewis's reactions to a *dead* spouse, when life is all we are letting ourselves think about here. But you were absolutely right to send it. I guess you know, although I don't know how, that it is not the process of Meg's dying that I fear. I hate that, but I don't fear it. What I fear is afterwards. Being married, having been married for twenty-nine years, the expectations, obligations, routines of being married, that great shared backlog of experiences, humor, etc.—this has always fueled and consoled me more than anything else in my life. My closest friends here say I am a schoolaholic, an updated, rather more reflective Mr. Chips, but they are dead wrong. As I've often told you—and meant it—I have retained my objectivity about, and respect for, school as well as I have chiefly because something deep within me still dreads school, is afraid of it and its demands. My thirty-two years' accrued experience has produced only the thinnest, most uneasy kind of confidence. Like a farmer who has not yet lost a harvest but who is working an ancient flood plain, I know that the worst can always happen. I have seen it happen in a classroom, and I have felt it threaten, but not quite bring down, a whole school. It begins in some hard-to-define chemistry of morale: bad feelings between faculty or between faculty and some students. Then some dramatic events may occur. They can be unrelated, like an accidental death or a fire or a disciplinary crisis. And then suddenly—poof! Nothing feels right at school. Nobody is reassuring or believable. If you're on the bottom, people on the top seem nervous and tentative. If you're on the top, you feel unsupported and unappreciated. There is no longer the corporate confidence that is so necessary to personal confidence and growth. *That* is what seems always to be lurking just below the surface of school life, and that is what I would be perpetually afraid of, were it not for Meg, whose company is more reliable, more familiar, a balm. School, although through the gate and along the path, is Away. Meg is Home. So again, what I fear is the loss, not the losing, which is still practically having. And this is what Lewis addresses directly.

My perspective is perhaps not right just now, but isn't this an odd piece for Lewis? I have always liked his voice very much. He has always represented to me the hearty, thinking, man's-world Englishman with his pipe. But the voice in *A Grief Observed* is not only muted and bereft, it never picks up. He still seems lost at the end. I suppose I read the piece thinking he is going to put the Event in a framework that makes everything mean something, and through that meaning, more comfortable. But he doesn't. Maybe he does, but I am too numb and lazy these days to work through any theology, even his. In spite of my deep, unworked-through conviction that our skeletal religious services at school add something important to school life, I have never managed to bring myself face to face with proper religion. I let my childhood church-going habits erode away, without regret, in college, and that pretty much has been that. Occasionally a good writer will puff something numinous into an old ember, but I don't let it come to much. I suppose I know that to take the Western faith seriously, I would have to reorder my relationship to everything, and I feel too old and too weak for that—but not too wise. Moreover, I think that to seek heaven's comfort at this particular moment, given my sustained lack of interest during good times, would be rather too much like the grasshopper and the ants. I know I would feel as pitiful and wretched as I am sure that pack of grasshoppers feel who ran out from under Nixon when he was finally turned over. I don't think I want to be Born Again. I only want to live properly.

Actually, honestly, the only thing I am really committed to now is seeing Meg through this thing. After that, I have no ambitions. Doesn't sound as if Lewis had any, either. Incidentally, she is hanging in there nobly, although it is depressing to be enervated and ill for such a long time. She has been without real energy for several months now. Still no eating, her weight is in the nineties, and there's some real discomfort in her guts and lower back. I know she is still sustained by reading and corresponding. A Levin letter ranks highest in her postal intake.

We still cannot find Brian, which is her major (unstated) worry and disappointment. For my part, I move in and out of cycles of paternal worry and depthless anger—which is possibly why he is continents apart. I think I still love Brian, at least love my composite recollection of him. I do not love his generation, its style, any of its novelties and contributions to the culture. I don't even know, for instance, if his prodigality is based on family tensions, or on unknowable archetypal rites of passage, or

on drugs. Of course it lets me off the hook to believe it is
in large measure the latter, but I really think that is the
case. I do. Meg and I have of course been guilty of
parental excesses, mainly excesses of ambition for Brian,
but surely these have been excesses within the normal
range. After all, we're not freaks. Everybody agrees we
are pretty nice. My nephew Hugh, an exact contemporary
of Brian, thinks I am infallible. I half expected Brian's
acting out in school, even urged him not to attend Wells,
and urged him several times to leave it, but he was
adamant. I have never minded anger much, or open
rebellion, or even looniness from him, but what has
paralyzed both of us has been his fuzzy-headed, hip passivity.
Baxter, our school shrink, says it's Passive Aggression. I
think it's passive aggression extended chemically by his
damned pot and God knows what else. As a young man,
Brian is a poorer reasoner—simpler—than he was as a
twelve-year-old. Whatever part drugs have played in Brian's
development, they haven't helped. And although I haven't
mentioned this to Meg, I am sure he has found his
narcotic heart's desire in North Africa. If drugs had been
around (perhaps they were), I wonder if the real prodigal
son, or Absalom, or any of them would have come back.

What a long, irritating, self-centered letter I've written.
Sorry, but thanks.

Tell me what you are reading, and send me some
poems. I am working on a long, slightly shapeless piece I
want you to see. It's about *having* cancer, interior view.
I'll send it along as soon as there are any contours. It is
still O.K. not to pull any punches. I'll write and tell you
when I'm too tender for that.

Best,

J.

Mr. Frederick Maitland
Headmaster, St. Ives Academy
Derby, Connecticut

Dear Fred,

Thanks for your letter.

Having said as much as I have already said on the subject, I cannot see the point of going over the situation again. I can't determine whether you don't see my point or whether you merely don't agree with it. I think I have stated our position clearly.

Dewey Porter has called me to say he will be glad to put a uniform code of athletic conduct at the top of the Seven Schools agenda in November. As I indicated to you earlier, I think such a discussion should be promising and is somewhat overdue.

You are mistaken, I think, to assume that it is a Seven Schools decision whether we drop St. Ives from our athletic schedule. While that prospect may well be a Seven Schools concern, it is a Wells School decision. It is a decision, moreover, that we have already, reluctantly, made. We have made arrangements to play St. Francis Priory both home and away next fall, instead of just once, and that fills our fall program. Although you have every right to protest this at the Seven Schools meeting, I assure you our decision is firm. You may want to cover your own schedule for September as soon as possible, as I am sure you know how frustrating it is trying to drum up fall contests, especially football games, after the season has passed.

I am sorry the Wells-St. Ives rivalry has had to be interrupted in this manner. Doing so is unsatisfactory in many respects. But I still maintain the principles at issue warrant the decision, and it is one I will be glad to justify to any and all concerned.

As a courtesy to you, I am informing you of our decision to cancel, for an indefinite period, our athletic contests with St. Ives before announcing it to our student body and larger school community. I think it would be a shame for you somehow to "hear" what we have done.

Again, I regret that this course of action is necessary. The athletic staff and I will be glad to meet with you at your convenience, before or after the Seven School meeting, to discuss the future of the athletic relationship.

My good wishes,

John

6 October

Mr. William Truax
President, The Fiduciary Trust Co.
P.O. Box 121
New Haven, Connecticut

Dear Bill,

Thanks for your note.

Three things:

1 • I will prepare for Friday's finance meeting several potential budgets for next year, showing implications of greater and smaller enrollments, also showing the implications of reducing staff. Capital and maintenance figures have to project estimated inflation rates, so I can't see trimming there. Agree?

2 • I am afraid that in the Opening-of-School Crush, the "Wells: Ten Years and After" study has been placed temporarily on a back burner. We have collected some data from faculty, though, and hope to have something concrete to report by the fall board meeting in November.

3 • You may or may not have heard about the ruckus surrounding our football opener with St. I. A very bad show: dirty playing, punches flying, cursing (which provoked an unattractive, anarchic crowd response). We benched some players. St. I. didn't. The officials lost control over the game. (And we got thrashed.)

I wrote to Fred Maitland asking for support in address-ing the problem—and was surprised not to get it. The subsequent correspondence you have seen. Unable to get even an *acknowledgement* from Fred that the opener represented a sorry spectacle, we've dropped them from our program, at least for next year. There is already some stink about this. And I suspect you'll hear some, too, mostly from older Wellsians who like the cowboy approach to sport and who remember when...

So be forewarned.

Meg and I both appreciate your family's concern and the gorgeous flowers. She is doing remarkably well, feisty, funny, tired of being sick.

Best,

John

7 October

MEMO to Tim Shire
Master of Hallowell House
(Personal and Confidential)

Tim—

See no reason to be cautious here. Even if we overreact we will do ourselves a service, especially considering the time of year. The early indications, if true, sound horrendous.

Remember to interview the boys separately and to *keep them separate,* until you have finished. Each has no idea of what the other has said—and thus may more easily imagine he is cooked and thus may come clean sooner.

Meanwhile I'll be in touch with the police and see what counsel they offer and what our obligations are.

Come see me, with or without culprits, when you have

talked to the boys. I don't mind the hour. I will be up late.

I naively hoped that this sordid phase of the era was behind us. Guess not.

J.O.G.

7 October

Mr. Frank Greeve
14 Bingham Drive
Tarrytown, New York

Dear Frank,

Thanks so much for taking the time to follow up on your English friend's tip. I will write M. Baddely at the British consulate in Tangier and see what transpires. I am surprised at the number of young American "transients" your friend estimates are billeted there. Soon I will cease to be surprised by anything.

Meanwhile, I am smack in the middle of—guess what— another suspected boy-drug ring. What a hopeless, irritating, criminal waste of time all this is. Apparently there is no end to this particular cultural development. What can your stereo do? What can your Harley-Davidson do? What can your Trans-Am do? What can your head do? How did altering feeling states by technological and chemical means *ever* get established as a good idea? What a culture.

Meg is stable, but awfully thin and awfully low. She is hurting physically but won't say much about it. I'm afraid it's a bad time ahead. She doesn't seem to be able to, or to want to, *initiate* as much talk and activity as she did even a couple of weeks ago. I don't think she has the energy.

I believe I'm learning a little bit about how life works. It is appetite: intellectual, sexual, esthetic, gastronomical. Subtract these, one by one, and life is diminished proportionately. The last thing to go, and it seems to go quickly without the rest, is a kind of critical self-awareness. That's Meg; she is past wanting now. She only registers. I have heard about remissions and improvements, and I am waiting.

That will have to do. I have, as I have said, this mess in the wings. Love to Val and Hugh.

John

REMARKS TO THE SCHOOL

By now some of you have heard that there is an important disciplinary inquiry afoot. To stifle rumors and hurtful speculation, I want to tell you this morning that, yes, there is an important disciplinary inquiry afoot. As the situation stands this morning, we have learned the following:

A sixth former in Hallowell, Steve Pennington, apparently made arrangements this summer to have his brother mail him a sizable quantity of LSD to be passed on, at a price, to interested Wells boys. The shipment seems to have arrived in Monday's mail, and Steven sold some of the LSD to two other sixth formers, Charles Stone and Terry Wilcox; to a fifth former, Ed Hruska; and to a third former, Marc Slavin. Over a long afternoon yesterday and a good part of last night, the five boys just named were questioned by Mr. Shire and by me, and each has admitted to as much as I have told you. Some remaining LSD and the money paid for it have been collected by Mr. Shire. The boys have been in touch with their parents by telephone, as have I. Student-Court proceedings will begin when this assembly adjourns.

At present, we are not sure we have confiscated all the LSD that was mailed here Monday, and we are not sure that only five boys were involved. If there are others of you involved, I invite you to turn yourselves in to me or to your housemaster. Given the nature of the offense, I cannot compromise punishment, or even assure you that you will not be dismissed from the school. I can promise, however, that if what we learn about your involvement in

46

this business comes from a voluntary admission from you, and not as a result of cross-examination or detection by us, things will go better for you than otherwise. You have my word on that.

This is somber news to start the day with, and I am sorry to have to bear it. I doubt that any of you, considering what we have written to your families and what has been said repeatedly from this stage, are in doubt about our drug policy. It's a very easy policy to remember: there is to be positively none of it here, under any circumstances. Over the past two years, every boy caught using, exchanging, or found under the influence of drugs at Wells has been dismissed. In other words, we could not be more serious about our drug policy.

Whether or not you agree with it, our policy has become what it is because of our actual experience here over the past two decades. There was, at the beginning, real confusion about drugs, confusion about *if* drugs were a problem and confusion about what sort of problem they were. We are no longer confused. We have had a good deal of experience now of students who smoked pot, took pills, inhaled cocaine, and so on, and as I say, we are no longer confused. Some of us here can remember school when there were no drugs whatsoever on the scene, except liquor which, killer and thief of human promise that it is, has at least been a familiar part of the social fabric of Western life since antiquity. As I say, some of us were working here before the drug scene, worked here through the early days of the drug scene, and are still here. The changes we have seen in drug-using boys are uniform. Let me summarize them as I see them.

1 • They do poorer school work and less of it than formerly; never better and more.

2 • They drop team and other organizational commitments; never add team and other organizational commitments.

3 • They initiate less activity not connected to getting and using drugs.

4 • They are harder to interest and to arouse.

5 • They care less about non-drug-taking friends, about family, and about others in general than they did before their involvement with drugs.

6 • They do not perceive or attach feelings to dramatic personal and academic losses and may even claim that they are functioning better and thinking more clearly than before.

7 • They increasingly organize themselves socially around drug taking and associate predominantly with other drug-taking friends, even when there is no other basis of shared interest than drugs.

Schools, even this one to a degree, have been changed by the presence of drugs. This is difficult to be precise about, but without question faculty-student trust has been diminished since the onset of casual drug use by the young. By the very nature of the activity, students are unable to be truthful to parents and teachers about drugs. Student communication about drugs is necessarily private and furtive. Similarly, drugs are purchased and property exchanged for them in a clandestine manner, involving, often, theft and dishonesty.

At the national, aggregate level, aptitude-test scores have declined every year since psychoactive drugs have been on the scene. Moreover, the number of adolescent suicides and serious crimes has risen geometrically since the advent of casual drug use, just less than a generation ago. Marijuana and other psychoactive drugs are now the leading cause of referral to mental health treatment centers for the young. I have known *scores* of happy and functional families torn apart by drug use of a teenage member or members. I have known some of these families intimately; one of them, quite intimately. I know of no family or school where the corporate life has remained unaltered or been improved by drug use.

Nationally the drug culture is supporting a multi-billion dollar industry controlled increasingly by organized crime. Several South American and Central American governments have been reorganized in a disturbing manner to accommodate the booming U.S. drug trade.

And for what? A chemically induced, acutely toxic thrill? Pleasure? Pleasure at those costs? No society organized around the pursuit of here-and-now pleasure has sustained itself. I would be pleased if some of you history scholars would take time to test that hypothesis.

Have I carried things too far? Possibly exaggerated to make my point? I wonder. Frankly, I wonder. But this much I can say for certain: drugs have occasionally hurt Wells School—hurt individual boys, hurt our corporate trust, hurt our general morale. Drugs have hurt us when boys have been caught, and they have hurt us when boys have not been caught. You know this as well as I do.

And now we have Mssrs. Pennington, Stone, Wilcox, Hruska, and Slavin on the line. Five promising souls. Five boys I happen to like. And who knows who else?

I would like to close by advising you gentlemen that I have unlimited time on my hands for discussing any of the things I have just said. Please come by if you are concerned, angry, or just want to talk. I can't think of anything in the history of this school more important to talk about.

I think I'll leave it there. Report to first hour classes. All classes through midmorning break will be shortened by ten minutes.

Good morning.

9 October

MEMO
To All Faculty

Dear Colleagues,

I am afraid there is no softening the news: it's time for fall-term advisor letters. Since I have never been able to figure out how so many of you find the time to write them as extensively and as thoughtfully as you do, I shall cease to try. Rather than set firm deadlines by form, let's establish that all of them should be submitted to Marge no later than a week from Friday. I cannot set the date any later and still leave time for any parental correspondence and student improvement before the end of the term.

Please make them as presentable, grammatically correct, etc. as you can. If in doubt about the boy's schedule or family set-up, please consult files. By all means let's avoid cheerily addressing deceased parents, or remarried parents by former names. (The problem is, they always call *me* to complain; not, however, the deceased ones.)

One more thing: whenever possible, when communicating a problem to parents, indicate the problem *behavior* and not just the judgment. "One out of three homeworks not turned in" conveys more than "erratic" or "lazy." If you are talking about someone's rudeness or insensitivity, recount some of the things the boy has said and done in its context. If possible avoid, "he is _____" in favor of "I am seeing a great deal of _____."

I thank you in advance for your hard work. These letters are without question our most important school-home link.

J.O.G.

10 October

Mr. Jake Levin
R.D. 3
Petersfield, New Hampshire

Dear Jake,

I have enclosed my "cancer" poem (unfinished) for your consideration. It may interest you solely because of its discontinuity from anything else you have seen from me. Whose voice is that, anyway? I had the weird feeling, while working on it, that it isn't mine. A good shrink could tell me, I am sure.

Anyway, I'll be glad to have your appraisal. I know it's morbid. Is it anything else?

Everything is high-speed and fuddled here. The prospect of telling you my news exhausts me. Suffice it to say that school is noise, Meg is having a hard time. O for the peace that surpasses all understanding shantih shantih shantih, etc.

J.

CANCER

This sooty film over the tree line,
Over shops, over traffic,
These wires slung, netted over the intersection,
Here, where we are, idling in these fumes—
Is this new territory?

Do I or does my cancer see
The long-legged woman in the sheer dress;
Hear the click of her step on the pavement?
Is it all spoiled?
Have I spoiled it?

What has come over me?
My schoolgirl asks.
Cancer, my Death's head replies.
O rose, thou art sick.
I am failing, slightly, to replicate.
I am a ruined autocracy.
I imagine cold efficiencies in my lymph,
The reorganization already silently underway.
What fear swells in the throat is superstition here;
Prayer a quaint tradition.

For the time being
This voice at least is mine.
If you will listen, please,
You will hear where I leave off,
Where cancer begins its song or songs.

You are the devil, cancer.
You are legion,
Without passion, demoralizing
Me, my family, all of us—
Is this you speaking already?

No. Cancerous, I can chronicle,
Be true as I can be
To this mute pathology.
It's important to be true,
And there is nothing else to do.

Your first question: how it *feels*.
One feels it very little—
A wan nausea
Which may very well be fear.
You've felt worse. Fatigue.

Perhaps later the flesh will startle.
What startles now is circumstance:
Regardless April is on again,
Sunny, softening up the land,
And geese are pleased enough to swim the cemetery
    pond.

All the quiet of a long day home
I muse in a museum of stale concerns:
In this very chair I have cared
Effusively about termites in the porch,
Conceived of, *dared* a station wagon,

Shaped, reshaped pictures
Of the same income and assets,
Looked to the cosmos for grounds for hating the chain
    saw,
Daydreamed myself entering, well-dressed and glib,
The parlors of the illustrious.

Now small narcissisms
Play about a more compacted world:
Something familiar in my fuss
About vegetables and vitamins,
Costs and benefits of a new chemical.

If I lose my hair to radiation,
I may win six odd, tuft-headed months.
I would read one hundred fifty books,
Hear traffic—and yes, and yes—
Behold in cancer twilight beloved faces.

(IN PROGRESS)

_____

11 October

Mr. and Mrs. George F. Pennington
3 Bay Road Circle
Wellesley, Massachusetts

Dear Mr. and Mrs. Pennington,

I am writing to confirm officially the sad and frustrating news I conveyed to you over the phone last night: that on the recommendation of the Student Court and of the Faculty Discipline Committee, I have decided to ask you to withdraw Steven from Wells immediately.

I write this knowing full well the unhappiness this event has caused and will continue to cause in your family. But given the nature of the offense—bringing dangerous drugs into the school and selling them—there is really no alternative. To take any other course would be to disregard the welfare of, and to confuse, the rest of the school community.

I have always liked Steven and have found him a game, if not an inspired scholar, and an interesting conversationalist. I would not dare or care to assess whether his academic slump over the past few terms is related to involvement with drugs. Perhaps, though, this is a question you may want to pursue as a family.

Boys make mistakes, even very serious mistakes, and some boys rebound and learn from them. I have every confidence that Steven can get back on the track. I also hope this sad incident provides him a sufficiently dramatic occasion to separate himself from psychoactive drugs and everything to do with them.

My secretary, Marge Pearse, will send Steven's transcripts to whatever school or schools you indicate. Please address such inquiries and related material to her attention.

It is hard for us, too, to lose a sixth-form boy, in whom we also have invested much.

Sincerely,

John O. Greeve

11 October

To the Parents of:
Charles Stone (6th)
Terry Wilcox (6th)

Dear Mrs. Stone/Dr. and Mrs. Wilcox,

I am writing to confirm officially the upsetting news I conveyed to you over the phone last night: that on the recommendation of the Student Court and of the Faculty Discipline Committee, I must ask you to withdraw ———————— from Wells immediately.

I write this knowing full well the unhappiness, to say nothing of the inconvenience, this causes in your household, but given the nature of the offense, there can be no alternative. In spite of clear and persistent cautions about drug traffic here, ———————— arranged to purchase, did purchase, and apparently used LSD at the school.

Wells School has not always been a happy experience for ————————. He has been on disciplinary probation within the last year, although not for this term, and he has generally impressed us as a boy who seeks his fun and solace outside the realm of schoolwork and activities.

It was not our business to investigate the extent of

————————'s involvement with drugs, but from various statements made to both the Student Court and to the faculty committee, the involvement seems to be extensive and various. Neither ———————— nor his friend ———————— expressed any contrition about the course of recent events, which may be a defensive pose. It may also be a serious concern. In my experience here many boys have rebounded from trouble, even serious trouble, but I have rarely—in fact, never—known one to do so while still involved in psychoactive drugs.

My secretary, Marge Pearse, will send transcripts to whatever schools you indicate. Please address such inquiries and related materials to her attention.

I close this letter with honest regret, but also warm hopes for brighter days on ————————'s horizon.

Faithfully,

John O. Greeve

11 October

Mr. and Mrs. Gabriel Hruska
5560 Ledgehill Road
Danbury, Connecticut

Dear Mr. and Mrs. Hruska,

I am writing to confirm officially what I told you over the phone last night: that I have accepted the Student Court's and faculty's recommendation that we ask you to withdraw Ed from Wells immediately.

I know this decision has saddened and upset the Hruska household. It has saddened and upset Wells, too. As I wrote you last spring, I really thought that Ed was over the hump and would succeed here. I am practically certain that he was free of drugs during all of last year, and his impressive academic turn-around shows it.

One of the reasons I regret seeing Ed go is the loss to our community of a family like yours. You have been uniformly forthright and supportive in all of your dealings with us. No family in my memory has shared more thoroughly their son's past history, "warts and all." What hurts so much about this incident is that I know how much you were counting on Wells School as a place where Ed could be free from old troubles. Sometimes I wonder if there is any place in the United States where Ed could be free from those influences. I wish Wells were such a place, but apparently it is not.

For what this observation is worth, it is my opinion that Ed was not really very close to the other boys involved in the LSD business. Three of the others are a form ahead of him, and as Ed admitted, they took little interest in him beyond his being a potential customer.

I hope this latest mess is what Ed needs to get fed up with the secretive, shoddy, outlaw world of youthful drug use. I think it just might be.

I agree with you, by the way, that the high school is the best idea. Among other things, he will find himself, I think, a relatively strong student there academically. You may contact my secretary, Marge Pearse, for his transcript.

I wish all of you well, and I hope this is not the last I hear of the Hruskas.

My good wishes,

John O. Greeve

11 October

Mr. and Mrs. Samuel Slavin
1300 Chafee Circle
West Hartford, Connecticut

Dear Mr. and Mrs. Slavin,

I am writing to confirm officially what I told you over the phone last night: that I have reluctantly accepted the Student Court's and the Faculty Discipline Committee's recommendation to ask you to withdraw Marc from Wells immediately.

I know this is devastating news, and it is truly unpleasant news to bear. For what the admission is worth, Marc's was the only recommendation concerning the five boys involved in this incident that I was seriously tempted to reverse. On his side is his newness to the school, the obvious temptation to play up to big, influential upper formers, and of course his extraordinary intellectual promise. Overriding these considerations, however, is the impact of "pardoning" him on the eighty-nine other boys in the third form. I don't want to lose any more boys here to drugs. In order not to, I need to create a climate of opinion in which drug use is "dangerous." We have evolved the drug policy we now have because we have learned, painfully, that the use of psychoactive drugs by adolescent boys is dangerous to development, although not always in ways boys can see and accept.

I am not sure how deeply Marc is involved with drugs. I was interested to learn that he is no novice. I honestly hope this incident is sufficiently dramatic for him to reconsider what he is doing and to get free of drugs and their social props. If he is able to do this and if he is so inclined, I invite him to come see me in June and to convince me that he should have another shot at Wells. I would gladly be convinced—and will save him a place in his form, at least through June.

Please address correspondence about Marc's transcripts and records to the attention of Marge Pearse, my secretary.

I am sorry things have taken this turn. May brighter things lie ahead.

Sincerely,

John O. Greeve

MEMO to Arnold Lieber
Maintenance

Arnold,

Just visited by coaches Shire, Menotti, Griffin, and
Deveraux. They say there are *no* lines whatsoever on the
soccer fields. They also say you *won't speak to them* when
they approach you about it. Odd behavior, Arnold.

Lines down *today,* please.

JOG

12 October

MEMO to Florence Armbruster
Mathematics

Dear Florence,

The Student Court has just referred to me a disciplinary decision involving your fourth-form geometry section.
I plan to do as you recommend, but I would like you to
give some more thought to the idea of "collective" discipline.
Funny things get done and felt when a whole class is
uniformly punished for an unadmitted, unassignable offense.
The guilty party remains ornery and convinced that justice is blind—and so do the innocent majority. Very often
nobody is happier or better off, and the tone of the
classroom does not improve.

For now the detentions stand as assigned. Care to
confer?

JOG

The Rev. Clive Clague
Rector, St. Christopher's Church
Middlebury Center, Connecticut

Dear Mr. Clague,

Many thanks for your extraordinary talk about the meaning of Gothic in the Middle Ages and after. That is not a subject I would have bet would enthusiastically engage the whole school, especially under formers, but how wrong I would have been. I am always delighted when our boys confront a lively intellect and a well-developed esthetic sense in somebody who is not a teacher. In a boy's mind, teachers are paid to try to be that way. In anyone else the qualities must be genuine, perhaps even valid.

Please find enclosed our modest honorarium. By no means does it represent the extent of our appreciation. It comes with our warm regards, though, and an open invitation to return soon.

My good wishes,

John O. Greeve

13 October

Mr. Robert Miravelli
Miravelli and Associates
2490 Boylston Street
Boston, Massachusetts

Dear Mr. Miravelli,

I am sorry not to have responded sooner to your letter of last week, but there has been much more than the usual crush of work here.

I am decidedly not in a position to have my portrait painted at this time. Traditionally, I believe, the directors of a school, or at any rate someone other than the subject himself, commissions a portrait of the headmaster. In this regard, I bow to tradition.

Sincerely,

John O. Greeve

15 October

Mr. Dewey Porter
Chairman, Seven Schools Conference
Adelbert School
Eavesham, Connecticut

Dear Dewey,

Thanks for your letter and for the proposed agenda for November.

If I hadn't been preconditioned by what I found to be an incomprehensibly dim correspondence from Fred Maitland, I think your response to our tiff with St. Ives would have surprised me. Of course we would be glad to talk about it; we look forward to it. But we are not in a position to reconsider our decision to drop St. I. from our schedule, at least for a year. The reasons are pretty clearly set down in the correspondence I sent you. At any rate, we have already adjusted our own schedule. Deed's done.

The question you posed—do we intend to drop all opponents whose sportsmanship falls below standards—is an interesting one, and I choose not to take it rhetorically. I would certainly like to drop opponents, all of them if it came to that, who refuse to acknowledge play as blatantly dirty and unsportsmanlike as we experienced in our opener with St. I. That is not a fine distinction. What I wanted from Fred was just an *acknowledgement,* so that we could address our respective teams and schools appropriately. When this is no longer an obvious course of action, I for one am ready to drop interscholastic athletics altogether.

Nothing could be further from my intentions than to "one-up" St. I. If anything, we are quite publicly one-down. We lost the game, we lost the brawls, and, for the time being, we have lost a time-honored athletic rival.

I wish you had seen the game, Dewey.

Sorry not to be more helpful. I look forward to seeing you soon.

Best,

John

16 October

Mr. and Mrs. Frank Greeve
14 Bingham Drive
Tarrytown, New York

Dear Val and Frank,

Thanks for your good, warm letter.

I don't think your visit tired Meg. I think it stimulated and touched her, although she has a hard time registering that through the discomfort. She is not distressed by the people who visit, but by being unable to respond to them appropriately. But it's still Meg in there, and she loves both of you fundamentally.

It's been a bad week, to tell the truth. Meg is very uncomfortable, depressed, and unable to sleep. Part of this I am sure has to do with the hospital. I know I am no one to speak, with my polite humanities education and having come of age before the technological behemoth of modern medicine, but Meg's regimen in the hospital is patently hopeless. Everything about the place is a confirmation of her disease. Except for her flowers, redolent of pity and utterly alien in the off-white, waxy confines of a hospital cell, there is nothing to engage eye, ear, or imagination, nothing except the hospital's own business. There is no privacy, no quiet. The rate for the room alone, without medicine and specialists' fees, is $325 per day. The only responsible alternative is to have her home here with round-the-clock nurse's care. This course, which may be more humane, is less expensive, but not coverable by medical insurance. It would break our little bank to bring her home, but I am glad to do it. My only worry is that I won't be able to keep this place peaceful enough. I've let it get a little Grand Central-ish since Meg's been gone. I suspect I could reverse that. The other problem is that I've generated the useful fiction that Meg is only routinely ill. If she comes home, more friends will want to see her, which would further exhaust and sadden her. I don't want Meg to see her condition through the eyes of well-meaning but horrified friends. I guess I have to work this through. If I feel the same way in a week, home she comes.

Terrible letter! Sorry. I'd tell you a little about school, but it's no better at the moment.

Thanks for your wonderful offer to come up here with Hugh for a Thanksgiving do. I am going to decline it—for purely selfish reasons. Even being minimally festive and pleasant would take energy from me, and my humble pail is nearly empty. I conserve what I have by minimizing routines, especially social ones, and sacking out whenever I can. (I have slept the night in my clothes, by mistake, twice this week.) One side benefit is that I am slimming down nicely. I have a few alumni fetes to preside over— one of them in Philadelphia, the worst city in the world— but otherwise I plan to "crash," to use Brian's phrase, for as much of the Thanksgiving break as I can.

Best love to Hugh. I loved your account of his weekends on duty in the dormitory. Such is the case, I suppose, in small residential communities of healthy adolescent boys and girls. Why did anyone ever imagine it would be otherwise? "Love goes from love as schoolboys to their books," Shakespeare has Romeo say. As about everything else, the bard knew all about co-ed.

Love,

John

Mr. Calvin Kingery
Timothy Dwight College
1121 Yale Station
New Haven, Connecticut

Dear Calvin,

It is always good to see you, although some times more than others.

Tuesday was one of the others. Needless to say, I was disappointed by the program you and your Boolas gave us. You sang beautifully, all of you, and your presence on stage is impressive, but some of the material was inappropriate for us, and you know it. I cautioned you about "judgment" last spring when we confirmed the date, and Phil Upjohn said he spoke to all of you backstage and was given jocular assurance that all was going to be good clean fun.

I suppose if a similar group, without a Wellsian among them, had given us the same show, I would be less disappointed, but every bit as disapproving. Calvin, you *know* what goes and what does not go on our stage. Thanks to your program, some of our boys will undoubtedly claim precedent for various vulgarities they have been contemplating but not yet dared.

For what an old prude's opinion is worth, I think your group is too musically sound to rely on the vulgar stuff for audience response. It is easy to hear the difference between delighted laughter and embarrassed laughter. The former is better; the latter is easier.

So much from me. It must be reassuring for you to know that I haven't changed with the times. Incidentally, we were going to give the Boolas a modest honorarium of $150 to help defray travel expenses. But since you didn't quite keep your side of the agreement, I am donating it to United Way instead, on your behalf of course.

In spite of all this, I hope we see you here again soon, with or without your *Boolas*.

Faithfully,

John Greeve

63

17 October

Mr. William G. Truax
President, Fiduciary Trust Co.
New Haven, Connecticut

Dear Bill,

We are all set for the board, here, a week from Tuesday. Budget figures and other materials are in the mail today.

I'll be more than happy to set aside some open time to discuss the St. I. decision. I am not surprised there is some stink about it. I trust you would agree, though, that it's necessary stink. Leacock and Bolwell are old Ionians, are they not? Some things run thicker than principles... Don't worry, I'll be reasonable.

Best,
John

19 October

Mrs. Philip Stone
Honey Hill
R.R. 2
Bedford, New York

Dear Mrs. Stone,

There is no way, I suppose, to soften the hurt and bad feelings that follow the dismissal of a student, especially a sixth former, from school. I feel, however, that in Charles's case, those bad feelings may have distorted some important matters of fact. Whatever the source of the confusion, let me make the following matters clear:

1 • I made no disciplinary distinction between the boys who purchased the drugs and the boy who sold them, because both acts violate the very core of the school's drug policy. I simply don't believe that the buying/selling distinction is important. Without one, there would not be the other, either way. I am aware that the state and federal laws do draw a distinction, and I am also aware that according to every published measure of the

64

phenomenon, the state and federal laws have done nothing to curb rising drug use among the young.

2 • I am very sorry if anything I wrote or said over the phone gave you the impression that Charles did "nothing good" here. By saying his experience wasn't "entirely happy," I meant only that. I am glad that you and he feel there was so much that was positive in his career at Wells.

3 • I made no mention of reapplication for a later term or for a post-graduate year, because I don't think either course would be desirable, for Charles or for Wells. For Charles to return at some later point in the year after a stop-gap phase at another school would suggest our policy for upper formers who break major rules is to "rusticate" them temporarily. This is not our policy. We rarely take post-graduate students, and when we do, they are generally promising scholars who are either chronologically or physically young and who want another year's preparation and maturity before college. I don't think Charles needs such a year, here or elsewhere.

4 • I did not "humiliate" Charles and the other boys involved before the whole student body. I did state briefly what had happened and that Charles was involved. The boys admitted as much to the Student Court, to the Faculty Discipline Committee, and to their friends. Not to have announced to the assembled school what had happened would without question have given rise to speculation and rumor which would have been far more hurtful than the truth.

5 • I did not say, nor did I mean to imply, that I wanted "nothing further to do with" you or with Charles. I suggested that you deal with Mrs. Pearse directly only with respect to Charles's transcript. Mrs. Pearse serves as our registrar, and dealing directly with her saves a step, especially when I am out of town.

You mention that you are considering litigation. Of course this disappoints me, but you have every right to do it. It is hard for me to see the point of it. Charles not only had the "due process" of Wells School, he had it at its most deliberate and most caring. I for one would be pleased to stand by our treatment of Charles in court.

Respectfully,

John O. Greeve

19 October

Mr. William G. Truax
President, Fiduciary Trust Company
New Haven, Connecticut

Dear Bill,

I have this morning received a letter from a mother who says she might be interested in suing us in order to restore the dignity of her sixth-form son who was recently dismissed for purchasing LSD from another boy in Hallowell. My experience of such mothers and such letters is that the ominous hints rarely come to writs. Nevertheless, you might want to bounce her letter off Seymour to see what, as counsel, he makes of it. Just in case it comes to something, I am preparing a file of disciplinary memos, housemaster's notes, my address to the school, and all correspondence on the matter. I will make myself available to Seymour at his convenience, should he want more information.

Best,

John

21 October

REMARKS TO THE SCHOOL

Since you are subjected, from time to time, to warnings, reprisals, and corporate criticism from this stage, I thought it would be nice—and also appropriate—this morning to praise you. What in particular I would like to praise is

66

your exceptionally courteous reception of Mr. Ambioto yesterday in long assembly.

I will concede that his observations were a little specialized. Perhaps some general points might have been made before he plunged into the intricacies of East African partisan politics. His accent, too, made stretches of the talk hard to follow. The length of the talk was not, however, Mr. Ambioto's fault. He asked me how long he should speak, and I told him until he heard the carillon. Mrs. Pearse, however, was called away from her desk late yesterday morning, and the awaited signal never sounded. Thus Mr. Ambioto unwittingly gave us the longest continuous address ever delivered in Perry Chapel—perhaps the longest in the history of Wells. Entirely my fault, of course.

Anyway, from my perspective gazing out into all your faces, you looked a perfect sea of attentiveness and restraint. There was talk afterwards of growling stomachs, but none of this reached the pulpit.

So, three cheers for you, perhaps one or two for Mr. Ambioto, and none for Greeve. I suppose one should simply expect exquisite manners from Wells boys and say nothing about it, but I can't help it. You were easy to be proud of yesterday. My compliments and my apologies for the discomfort.

22 October

Mrs. Benjamin Rogen
46 Clubside Road
Newton, Massachusetts

Dear Mrs. Rogen,

Thank you for your letter expressing concern about Dan's situation in geometry.

I am glad you did not hesitate to write; dispel any notion about being considered a "Jewish mother"; I wish I knew how to *create* a Jewish-mother syndrome among our parent body.

With respect to geometry, I can only assure you that I am paying close attention, and will continue to pay close attention, to Mrs. Armbruster's mathematics sections. As it happens, she is not a "new teacher," but she is new to a boy's-school setting, and there has been a hiatus of several years since she last taught. I can assure you, on the basis of having seen her at work, that she is a well-prepared and competent geometry teacher. Geometry, however, involves a different mode of thought from algebra; it is not really an extension of algebraic thinking. It is not at all uncommon for a boy who, like Dan, has done well in algebra, to meet his match in geometry. It will come, I think, when Dan gets used to the structure of proofs. Battling Mrs. Armbruster, however diverting, is not going to help much.

About her alleged handling of discipline, I have only two things to say. One is that I have never heard (or, when I was in school, given) an uncolored account of an adversely experienced disciplinary decision. I do not doubt that Dan felt the tide of wrath and prejudice that he reported, but I am not sure that such things as he reported to you were actually uttered. Secondly, school's greatest contribution to an adolescent's personal development is certainly the variety of approaches to pedagogy and discipline that it offers. In the final analysis, Mrs. A. may not be for Dan, but I don't think I would want to save him from the battle. Our best experiences at school are not always our most pleasant ones. One more thing: the reported "chaos" of the geometry classroom cannot possibly be as reported. Phelps building is acoustically awful, and all of us would hear it!

I'm glad you got in touch. I will continue to monitor both Mrs. Armbruster's and Dan's progress in geometry with interest.

My good wishes,

John O. Greeve

MEMO to Florence Armbruster
Mathematics

Florence,

Let's confer.

J.O.G.

23 October

Mr. and Mrs. Frank Greeve
14 Bingham Drive
Tarrytown, New York

Dear Val and Frank,

Scheduling arrangements for the nurses (*five* of them) are now complete—a process much more demanding than hiring a faculty for the entire school—and Meg is home, relatively comfortable and relaxed in her own room. The maples are now practically bare, and the morning light from the big window in the bay nearly whitens the room. This is so obviously right I kick myself that we had it any other way. Dietrich and the clinic people, for their part, could not have been kinder or more obliging.

I honestly think this will give Meg more time—and better time. I was certain she had improved when, as I padded in quietly yesterday morning with coffee to join her for a chat, she perused me at some length in silence, then said, "You know, John, you look really awful. Are you well?"

Actually, I am quite well, although surprisingly trim. I am now belt hitches to the good of where I was on Labor Day. Do you think I should write this up and market it: How to Lose Fifteen Pounds without Dieting, through Stress, Overwork, and Dejection? A jog or two around the track to raise some color in my greenish, pallid cheeks, and I could get almost vain.

I am glad Hugh is heading down to Tarrytown for

Thanksgiving. Don't expect any company from him, however. If the standard pattern holds, he should come to you with a suitcase full of term exams to grade, grade reports to write, and advisor letters to compose. Give him my best, will you? I saw Ted Phillips at a Headmasters' Conference in Boston last week, and he confirms that Hugh is off to a marvelous start: careful, yet enthusiastic; high spirited with kids, yet very "adult." Have no doubt that as long as Hugh stays in schools, he will travel on the fast track.

Meg joins me in sending love.

John

25 October

REMARKS TO THE SCHOOL

First, let me thank you for saving me this important spot in your rally. I'm not sure I can rival captains Ted Frank and Carl Maslow for passion nor Coaches Shire and Kreble for determination, but I can serve you in two capacities: as an historian and as a prophet.

The historian in me insists that in order to make sense of these final contests with Haverhill, we must take a longer view than of just this season. For this season has revealed a very plucky, very young, rather unlucky Wells football team which has won only two games, while suffering six defeats. Two of those defeats were by less than a touchdown, and four games in all were lost during the last quarter of play. In contrast, Haverhill, my sources tell me, is riding the crest of the Seven Schools wave. They are undefeated. They have played only one close game this season, and they are, according to an inside source who cannot be named for reasons of his personal safety, complacent in the extreme about Saturday afternoon. In other words, we have got them where we want them. History would bear this out. In the forty-six years we have met Haverhill School in football, we have beaten them thirty-one times. They have returned the favor thirteen times, and there have been two ties. Of those forty-six contests, only twenty were played when Wells had a losing school record. Of those twenty games, Wells won thirteen, lost five, and tied two. This bears out an old and almost forgotten Wells School proverb which goes something like, "A strong Haverhill squad does not a Wells defeat insure." Words to that effect.

But as all you Western Studies scholars know, history is not the only source of knowledge. There is also direct revelation. Here too I have had access to well-placed sources. Last night I was unable to sleep and was nodding off fitfully at dawn when I detected a lightening on the horizon. Too early for the sun, I told myself, and sat bolt upright. Suddenly the room was aglow with light, and everywhere about me I heard the whooshing and flapping of invisible wings. Then lo, dark and quiet were restored, and all was as it had been, with the exception of a rectilineal luminescence glowing faintly on my pillow case. This was a sealed envelope which I picked up gingerly and which I will share with you this afternoon.

Please bear with me...

It seems to be a card, a blank card...no, there are some figures here...it says...it says...Haverhill 20, Wells 26. Extraordinary.

One more thing, boys, before we head out to fulfill this prophecy. It's trite—but still important—to remind you that how we do it is what matters, not what the scoreboard says. Many of you recall that this year's football season got off to a sour start at St. I.'s. That was a game I would like to forget, and my regret has nothing to do with the football. What I wish for all of us Saturday, players especially, is the indescribable elation that comes from pouring out best effort and energy. Anger, verbal abuse, and cheap shots have no part in this.

Finally, to our soccer and cross-country teams, already heard from, you need no prophecy from me to see your way to victory. What marvelous seasons you have both put behind you already.

The prospect of three fine wins on Saturday quite overwhelms me. I do believe I might be so undone by it that a full free day might be required for me to recover. The faculty and I hate to waste that good instructional time, but we shall just have to see what transpires.

Let's all of us, players and spectators alike, have a glorious weekend at Haverhill.

26 October

MEMO to Coaches
Kreble, Shire, Tomasek
Athletic Department

Just a note to wish you well at Haverhill and to thank you for your good, long efforts in conducting your teams through exceptionally classy seasons. It is easy to be proud of athletics at Wells this year.

One caution: not-so-veiled rumors are already rife among the players about the "traditional" post-season "bash." We have got to squash this. Let's find a minute to talk to the teams, preferably before the games, and drive home the point that we don't want to lose anybody at this point in the year to discipline or injury or something worse. I'll have a word with dormitory faculty on the subject, too.

Onward!

J.O.G.

26 October

Mr. Jake Levin
R.D. 3
Petersfield, New Hampshire

Dear Jake,

I am undone, feather-headed, and flattered. Unless you are a consummate con, you seem to be positively genuine in liking my "cancer" lines. I do not believe there is a precedent for this in our literary correspondence. Now that I think about it, the cancer piece is probably the only poetry I have ever shown you which is not in appreciation of something. What is it in me, do you suppose, that is unable to bring "energy and power" (your words) to appreciation, but able to find it for fatigue and fear? If you know, don't tell me. It must be horrible.

I am at home now in my study. Night is, I'd say, about five minutes away. A leaden blue-grey sky is softening even the leafless prickly treeline. Meg is asleep. Nurse McCarty (night shift Tues., Thurs., Fri.) is reading, or possibly drinking. All is quiet. And as the headmaster ponders the way of things in solitude, what does he ponder?

He ponders drinking and the problem of adolescent celebration in general. How did our social fabric ever get woven with such an annoying hole? Lest I sound obscure, the situation is this: our final games of the fall term are Saturday. Three teams have practiced and played hard, and some honest effort has been put forth, physical sacrifices made. Given the nature of the animals involved, the players have made an effort to keep the spirit of training regulations. Saturday night the boys would like, if they could arrange it without detection, to drink a lot of beer, to get loud and raucous and silly and, under that cover, be affectionate, sentimental, even ecstatic. For a few of the boys involved, the goal would be drunkenness and iconoclasm; for most of them it would be—though they'd die before admitting it—fellowship. But of course we can't have that, given school rules, state laws, *in loco parentis*, etc. And what a shame! What a sad restraint, a dreary response to some no doubt ancient, if not original, sin to do with drinking. I wish I could have the lot of them here in my parlor and not quite enough beer on tap to drown them. Did you know that used to be done? Remember that scene in *Tom Brown's School Days* when Tom first gets to Rugby? There is a huge anarchic football game, involving the whole school—a kind of free-form war organized around the movement of a ball. Tom does something minor but painful to advance his team's position. That night the *school* serves beer, and there is singing and speeches and (unmistakably tipsy) good fellowship before the porters turn off the taps. What has happened? What social progress has made this impossible?

You, on the other hand, are probably pondering the dual nature of the romantic ideal or the non-poetic poetics of concrete imagists or, more likely, a drink and some stew. Ah, the road not taken.

Thanks again for your warm and, as always, bang-on critical observations about the cancer thing. Finish it, yes. But have you thought about that? I can do cancer/despair by feeling it, by identification. But finishing it requires—well, being finished. Doesn't it? That I can't do vicariously. But I'll work on it; maybe I'll rely on Art.

We're managing here. The center is holding. Meg sends love. When next we meet, you will see a thinner, shored-up Greeve, a Greeve measuring 33″ around the waist, a diameter last recorded in his college days. Meg and my colleagues insist that I look godawful for the improvement, but I feel this is due to the way my old clothes hang about my no longer portly frame. Another theory, perhaps the valid one, is that I looked awful before and the recent difference merely points out a fact to which the dull-eyed faculty had become inured. It certainly is an interesting question, isn't it?

Don't forget about February. What are you reading? Writing?

Love,

John

30 October

REMARKS TO THE SCHOOL

I would like to conclude this morning's assembly by saying I am glad we won our contests with Haverhill. I cannot of course be as ecstatic as you are because, if you will recall, I knew we were going to win. Do not misunderstand me. I am not gloating. I take no personal *pride* in being prophetic. For prophecy, you know, is a gift. I am merely its location, its mouthpiece.

So in closing, let me repeat that I am very pleased with the fall teams, the way one is pleased that water falls or that a sail fills with wind. I would normally dismiss you for First Class, but I seem to recall a promise...

Now, you may either remain here in the assembly hall where some of the faculty and I have prepared a very informative program on seventeenth-century breakthroughs in natural science, or you may go off and do whatever you please. I believe cocoa and donuts are available in the Hall for anyone interested.

Good morning.

3 November

Mr. Dewey Porter
Chairman, Seven Schools Conference
Adelbert School
Eavesham, Connecticut

Dear Dewey,

Thanks for your letter. I agree—I think—that our session last week was productive, although the unstated "vibes" from Fred and the St. I.'s crew were a little chilling.

I like the proposed mechanism for settling sportsmanship disputes. The ad hoc ombudsmen should serve well, although if many protests are filed, their time may be heavily taxed. At any rate, I like it, I vote for it. I would have been glad to refer my St. I.'s tiff to such a board.

You ask me if I wouldn't consider, in the spirit of the new policy, reinstating St. I.'s on next year's schedule. Practically, I can't. We've already filled in most of the holes. Ethically, I don't think I would if I could. To relent at this point—still without an acknowledgement of foul play from Fred, I remind you—would hardly be in the spirit of the new resolves. I think we've got plenty of soft-headed accommodation these days, whether in national politics or in the schools. Why does a principle—even a well-established one—make everybody so uncomfortable? St. I.'s can just reschedule. Here I stand. (Did you know that Luther never said that?) I told Fred to get on that in early October. Now it's going to be tricky, especially in the fall.

Thanks for your kind words about our Haverhill triumph. I have nothing modest to say. I loved it.

Best,

John

5 November

Mr. Robert Lavell
CBS Television Network
51 West 52nd Street
New York, New York

Dear Mr. Lavell,

Thank you for your inquiry about Wells as a potential site for your *Here and Now* special, "The Last Boy's School."

I am afraid I must decline on the school's behalf. A school year, once in motion, establishes its own rhythm and momentum, and the to-do involved in being filmed might just spoil ours. Also, for whatever it says about us, we are rather avowed foes of television viewing. We do not recommend it in general, nor do we allow it here, either as a diversion or as a rival source of information to books and talk. We have no TV sets in our dormitories or in the lounges. Of course our policy reflects only our view of the relationship between TV and school; the larger question of TV's place in society is rather beyond us. In light of this, I don't think we would be very consistent in allowing ourselves to become an enthusiastic subject for television.

For what a personal observation is worth, my impressions, spotty as they are, of the *Here and Now* approach is that

76

the object is to "see through," debunk, or, at most, to reveal whatever is under scrutiny with such apparent detachment that the result is heavy irony. I may be mistaken in this, and, as I say, I seldom watch television. But has *Here and Now* ever celebrated its subject? If I were a skilled filmmaker and knew what I know about school life, I think I could make a documentary that would show *anything*. But what would be the point in that?

So, if not at Wells, I wish you luck with your project. And I hope you are able to celebrate what is fine in the school you ultimately settle upon.

My good wishes,

John O. Greeve

7 November

Mr. Hugh Greeve
Pembroke House
St. Edward's School
Framingham, Massachusetts

Dear Hugh,

Your letter positively hit the spot with Meg. The image of you working through the amorous entanglements (apparently I should use that term literally) of your dormitory charges is worthy of publication. Are you interested?

We regret, too, that a family "do" is not advisable for this Thanksgiving. Given Meg's energy level and the nature of her care, she could not really participate in any of the togetherness, and that would hurt her. Better, I think, to spend a quiet day with a warm picture of all of you in her heart.

I have looked forward to Thanksgiving recess more enthusiastically than I am to this year's, but I am nevertheless grateful for the breather. I have a mound of paperwork to do for the trustees and, frankly, I could stand to sleep for a day or two. Perhaps I'm getting old. I understand that school people in England can respectably retire in their mid-fifties, on the same principle that combat soldiers are allowed to be pensioned off early. But then what? Work for Jenkins in the boat yard in Sandwich? I may have to anyway if he charges anywhere near what he charged for the *Valmar* last winter. Why is it so expensive? They just put on varnish, don't they? I could put on varnish.

Still nothing from your wandering cousin, my son. We have some lookouts posted, though, on two continents.

Have a marvelous, restful holiday. I'll call your house Thursday p.m. Meg appreciates your writing even more for knowing the time of year and what you had to put aside to do it. In you, my boy, is the complete absence of everything I dislike in the young.

Love from both of us,

Uncle John

10 November

Mr. William G. Truax
President, Fiduciary Trust Company
New Haven, Connecticut

Dear Bill,

As promised after the board meeting, I am enclosing for you, and have already done so for Seymour, our complete records, including a chronology by me of the Charles Stone disciplinary proceedings. I am very sorry it has come to litigation. I can't imagine it will cost us anything, since, however marvelous their attorneys, there isn't much of a case for the boy. As I understand it, the Wilcoxes are attached to the suit just for the ride; Mrs. Stone is footing the bill. Seymour told me over the phone that damages have already been awarded in Connecticut to parties who have been shown to be "deprived of educational opportunity" after being "publicly" defamed by a school head. If this means that we can no longer address the school about important events in school life, the whole system has gone to smash. (Incidentally, I believe I have already sent you my remarks to the school on this matter.) I hope Tim Shire and I aren't tied up for days in court. I personally can't afford that at the moment, and Mrs. Stone does not deserve the satisfaction. You know it's historically true that every Western society from 4th century BC Athens to the present has been obsessed with litigation at the same time it has been in its most accelerated decline. The letter killeth, but the spirit giveth life. Bloody-minded woman.

I really appreciate your concern about Meg. You are by no means negligent in not inquiring sooner. I have actually taken some pains to keep the nature and extent of her illness something of a secret. This may not be fair to good friends, but it has served the narrower purpose of keeping both of our lives a degree calmer. We have not yet had to undergo the trial of seeing the sadness and fear reflected and magnified in the faces of everybody else we know. There will be a time for that, I am sure, but I am not quite up to it yet. For the present Meg will remain here at home under nurses' care. She is stable for the moment, although very weak and not very comfortable. It is the nature of this cancer that she has practically no natural resistance; hepatitis, pneumonia, or even a lesser virus is a greater immediate danger than the cancer.

Again, I am touched by your concern and by your generous offer to relieve me of school duties for an unspecified interim. For the time being, I would like to pass up that option. The rhythm of work at school is, besides taxing, also an ordering factor in my life. I'm not too proud to admit that I frankly need the work, for the time being. The alternatives terrify me, would bring me closer to what I dread most. Does this make sense? It is a relief to know, however, that if I should need to call on the board for some special dispensation in the months ahead, they may be favorably disposed.

I actually do have some unscheduled time opening up over the Thanksgiving Vac, and I will be able to devote some serious attention to "Wells: Ten Years and After." You have been patient with me on this, and I am grateful.

Because everybody else says so too, I will reluctantly have to accept your assessment of my physical appearance. I am not working myself ragged, I assure you. I think the real cause of my decline is the simple fact that I have reverted to a quite deeply ingrained seediness, veiled these long years from the general public's notice by fastidious adjustments on Meg's part. I am not "pooped," as you suggested last week. This is the real me. I looked the same—even weighed the same—when Meg lifted me out of my undergraduate pallor. I might remind you, too, that I am quite old, more the Barry Fitzgerald than the Bing Crosby in the Wells School saga. But again, I appreciate your concern. I will spruce and fatten up over the break. Who wants to be bad PR? Who wants to be pitiful? Not me. Although it might be effective to look a little beaten up in court when Mrs. Stone brings forth her venomous accusations.

I will keep in touch, Bill. I hope all of the Truaxes have a glorious holiday.

Best,

John

13 November

MEMO to All Faculty
Re: Term Exams

You will find attached the final version of the term-exam schedule we discussed at Friday's meeting. Unless there are excessive makeups, this schedule should allow ample time for exams to be graded before the holiday, which I sincerely hope is dedicated to well-deserved rest and diversion.

I would rather fuss about this too much than to commit

the other mistake. Please make a special effort to proctor these exams carefully.

1 • Do not leave exam copies on the copying machines or in wastepaper baskets.

2 • Do not allow boys to bring in anything but sharp pencils to the exam rooms (exceptions: art history, and Horney's history electives, for which special arrangements have been made).

3 • *Patrol* the exam room, don't merely watch.

4 • Take attendance as soon as boys are seated and quiet; report absentees to Marge at once.

5 • Do not make individual arrangements for make-up exams. Refer tardy or ill boys to proctor of the day (posted).

6 • Please be on hand at least fifteen minutes before exam is scheduled to begin.

It seems we lose a boy or two every year to cheating. Perhaps this is inevitable, but I hope not. Let's at least avoid fanning the flames of temptation. The better we monitor these exams, the easier it becomes to do so.

Thanks in advance for your care.

J.O.G.

15 November 19—

DRAFT of "Overview" to
"Wells: the Next Ten Years..."

A consideration of the next ten years of Wells School as a preliminary step to planning its longer-range future requires at least a cursory review of the school's history. We are not founding a school; we are attempting to be thoughtful custodians of what has been faithfully established at Wells over the past one hundred and six years. As we look to our future direction, we must be kept mindful that we are already on a course. We may choose to alter that course, but we would be unwise to abandon it without a careful assessment of where we have been and to what effect.

Wells was founded as a school for "boys of demonstrated promise who aspire to university training or for training in the practical arts." The founders also included in the school charter that "lessons of character, manliness, and Christian virtue" were to be undertaken in tandem with a program of "liberal arts and sciences." Although the student body has since grown from twenty-five to nearly four hundred boys, Wells has never significantly departed from these initial aims.

We are still a school for boys of demonstrated promise. One of a remaining handful of well-established boys' schools in the country, we carry on the traditions of male fellowship intended by the founders. While the current climate of opinion about the role of the sexes and their presumed interrelationship is tumultuous, and the social consensus about "a man's place" and "a woman's place" is no longer what it was when the school was chartered, a new social consensus has not yet emerged. While Wells School has increased significantly its coeducational functions, exchanges, and joint activities over the past fifteen years, its faculty and trustees and students have determined that a boys' school is still a satisfactory, and in a few respects superior, setting for assessing changing sexual expectations in the contemporary world. Moreover, Wells School has demonstrated that it is still a satisfactory, and arguably a superior, place to prepare for the intellectual challenge of college, and for adult life beyond. Moreover, our unusually loyal alumni body have supported the school in a variety of ways financially, and the larger community continues to send us more applicants for places than we can accommodate. We are fortunate to be working still with boys of "demonstrated promise." Over the past five years there have been more than four applicants for every available place, and last year the applicant pool was the largest it has been in a decade.

We continue to carry out our founders' charge to prepare boys "who aspire to university," although we no longer train many boys, at least directly, for the practical arts. Over the past decade every single Wells graduate has matriculated into college within a year of his graduation from school. Of last year's graduates, all but two matriculated into colleges and universities, and the two who elected to work and to travel for an interim period deferred until the following year places for which they had been accepted by colleges. Although a rigorous college preparatory school, Wells continues, in the context of contemporary society, to prepare boys for especially responsible work and for leadership, both of which were at the heart of the founders' stated aims.

Nor have we departed much from the ethical intentions of our charter: the "lessons of character, manliness, and Christian virtue." The lessons of character we convey in a number of ways. Foremost among these, certainly, is direct participation in school processes: captaincies, editorships, monitorships, prefectorships, Student Court, Student Senate, and the scores of other leadership opportunities and responsibilities every boy must to some degree take on. Moreover, we address students on points of character—on charity, on basic honesty—directly in assembly. There is also the required Ethics course for under formers, and optional ethics and religion courses for upper formers. So we not only insist on ethical conduct, we encourage serious reflection on ethical matters. Manliness we consider to be the expression of the fullest range of potential given to each man; it entails self-confidence, and self-confidence is impossible without genuine achievement. Seen this way, manliness is impossible without taking risks, physical, intellectual, spiritual, and emotional. Wells School unashamedly sets the standards and provides the challenges it does to invite risk-taking. Real risk-taking involves the possibility of failure. It is possible to fail at Wells. Typically, however, boys who fail are those who fail to take risks, who close themselves off from challenges. This is always regrettable, and for some boys only a temporary delay in development, but it is no basis, we believe, for lowering standards or for removing challenges.

Given the diversity of the Wells student body today—a pluralism both intended and welcome—it is no longer appropriate to restrict the kind of conduct we aim at to "Christian virtue." Wells has for the past fifty years been open to boys of all faiths and to those of no traditional faith. The standards of conduct expected and maintained are compatible, however, with all established religions. The school continues to hold a non-denominational assembly each morning, in which prayers are sometimes offered and in which inspirational addresses, including religious ones, are occasionally given. Sabbath services, including a non-sectarian Christian service in Perry Chapel, are encouraged but not required. A school chaplain is retained both as a teacher and as a pastoral counselor to all boys, whether Christian or not. While no longer a purely Christian school by composition or affiliation, Wells is still a school whose tone and student conduct are shaped by the religious tradition of our corporate past.

In many respects, then, Wells School continues to pursue the purposes originally set out for it. In so doing, the school is always in the process of carrying out two fundamental tasks—or perhaps two dimensions of the same fundamental task. We are simultaneously in the business of imparting to the young the best of our accrued culture ("a program of liberal arts and sciences") and of maintaining a humane, livable community. It is inconceivable that these two missions will not always be the primary business of a school.

In order to assess the future requirements of Wells in the coming decade and in the twenty-first century, it is necessary to scan the horizon for present or approaching realities that will either help or hinder Wells in carrying out those two essential missions. We must look to demographic developments and to every possible indicator of the state of the national economy. The availability and expense of ever scarcer fossil fuel on the eastern seaboard will without question affect the cost, enrollment, and— literally—the climate of the school. While we are monitoring actual and likely external developments, we must also take shrewd stock of internal needs. It is clear we must build, renovate and innovate in order to remain the same. Faculty salaries and benefits must rise with the current levels of inflation if superior instruction is to be maintained. The academic departments and the athletic staff have indicated below, in a ranked list, the major capital expenditures they feel would most enhance their respective programs. An ad hoc Student Life Commission has recently been established to generate a parallel set of recommendations from the students' perspective.

When these data are complete and assembled, they will be distributed to the various school constituents—students, faculty, board, alumni, parents—for further elaboration and refinement. Operating from these shared materials, we will begin to generate two programs. The first of these will be produced by the "immediate" constituents (faculty, students and parents) and should consist of those things most worthy of retaining in the Wells experience as well as those things most worth acquiring. From the board and alumni, we need to generate a program of *how* to retain and acquire these things. Central to both programs are the following questions:

1 • What is best and most durable about the Wells experience?

2 • What is worst and most expendable in the Wells experience?

3 • How might Wells be changed structurally and substantively to achieve its stated purposes?

These questions are very basic, but they should provide rich soil for argument and discussion. They are worth resolving since, provided for or not, the future will be upon us.

17 November

Mr. William G. Truax
President, Fiduciary Trust Company
New Haven, Connecticut
P.O. Box 121

Dear Bill,

Enclosed is a draft of an introductory statement to cover the "Wells: Ten Years and After" project. I have also appended some capital needs (or desires) compiled by the faculty, along with some population and demographic info I've culled from here and there. I would like to get a preliminary packet of such materials to the whole board, or at least to the Education Committee, as soon as you give me a green light.

Tell me what you think of this. I'm not sure.

To me, thinking about the future seems a strangely empty process. The only basis for imagination is the present and the past, which is obvious enough. But when you look to the present and the past for what is essentially good, you are accused of bone-headed conservatism. The accusation doesn't make any sense, but the alternative approach, a kind of compulsion to change, is clearly dominating the age. Futuristic visions are all grounded in a relatively shallow near-past. The daring edifices of Kennedy Airport look like a backdrop to a third-line science-fiction movie of the fifties. Boston's new harbor-end megaliths look like upended transistor radios. The most dated-looking buildings in North America are Frank Lloyd Wright's "modern" houses with their hideous overhangs and rectilineality.

What an anomaly, an absurdity to "plan" a future. The most glorious moments in Western history have come about by a confluence of accidents when men went energetically rummaging into the past, into prior traditions: New-Kingdom Egypt, Israel under David and Solomon, Periclean Athens, Augustan Rome, Carolingian Europe, Renaissance Italy, etc. Was Thomas Arnold a forward-looking headmaster? Boyden? Peabody? Have the greatest eras of any school's history been planned for? In the sense that Lockheed and Chrysler and the thousands of flash-in-the-pan government social agencies make their jargon-laden, scientistic long-range plans?

I for one would like to be able to make a plan to maintain Wells somewhere near its present level, but I don't have the "data" to do it. I think only God has the data.

Just grumbling, Bill. Pay no mind.

Best,

John

HEADMASTER'S NOTES
from *The Wells Quarterly*
Fall/Winter

It is the way of Fall Terms to be over before there is time to reflect on them, but we really should reflect on them, lest they lose meaning. Some great men who have thought about it seriously tell us that an event is most meaningful not when it is happening, but when it is recollected in tranquillity. I am not sure I can simulate tranquillity, but, for a day or two, as I write in this study in a boyless Wells, the world is at least relatively quiet.

The one hundred and sixth year looks to be a good one. We enrolled one hundred twenty new boys, ninety of them third formers, from the strongest applicant pool we have had since I have been at Wells. The boys remind me, with a corporate groan, that I tell them that every year. But it's true. "Hard" data, such as admission-test quintiles and school transcripts, bear it out.

Possibly because of the talented new boys at Wells or possibly because of the times in which we live—perhaps both—the academic pace of the school has markedly picked up. In faculty meetings there are persistent reports of difficult and sophisticated schoolwork being done, without carrots and sticks. Apparently the pursuit of scholastic

87

excellence gets a kind of guarded approval from today's young. This is a bright sign, insofar as the more we can enable boys with reasoning and general verbal skills, the wider will be the range of their pursuits and interests in the world beyond this little one. My own hardly stream-lined theory of adolescent learning is that if a boy can by whatever means—through a teacher's charm, through natural inclination, through early cultural stimulation, through a dull, persistent sense of duty, through fear— reach a certain critical level of verbal and logical proficiency, he has his papers for life into a comprehending, possibly intellectual, possibly appreciating adulthood. Short of this critical point, he closes off, perhaps makes polite gestures in the direction of "culture," but basically backs away from it as from a formidable alien.

To such souls life becomes, even at a relatively early age, a holding action. Such lives are dedicated to replicating what patterns of order they have mastered: boyhood pat-terns with adult props. Thus we see actual, chronological adults living for their place in the firm or the club hierarchy. They are obsessed with their leisure and sports because these things are not diversions from their life's work, they are *it*. Fuzzing experience or hopping it up or slowing it down through our great American array of alcohol and narcotics is another way, a chemical one, of maintaining old patterns against the terror and the prom-ise of new experience. It would not be a bad objective for Wells to be the kind of school that raised the suspicion among its students that the reward for submitting to disciplined thinking in school might be a sure place to stand in the staggeringly beautiful and complex swirl of creation. Insofar as the headmaster's musings are valid, perhaps it is an overall good thing that students are working hard. For our parts, we must be alert to any signs that it is uncritical, unplayful work or that it is unrelieved Pursuit of the Grade. (Although a little grade-consciousness, I've found, never hurt anybody...)

Athletically, we've had a mixed and really glorious term. *Tim Shire's* and *Dave Tomasek's* soccer and cross-country teams both cruised effortlessly—that is never strictly true—to Seven Schools championships, the third straight in soccer. Lineman *Theo Lederer* set a new Wells record for season goals in soccer and was named, along with *Rusty Drakeman* and *Chub Latta,* to the all-division first team. (For more details and season highlights, see the Sports Wrap-Up, pp. 28-30.) The real athletic treat of the season—and for some of us, of our careers—came courtesy of *Jack Kreble's* not-so-winning, but explosive football team, which managed to close its season by "upsetting" (not my word) an undefeated Haverhill team, 20-12. A large, boisterous Wells crowd, most of them less prescient than their headmaster, felt our boys acquitted themselves admirably by staying within range of the awesome Haverhill, 0-12 at the half. But then. Few of the fans, and none of the players will forget it. The experience was framed by a glorious, cold, clear afternoon (and by Wells soccer and cross-country wins). How like story books for boys is life in a school for boys.

If I may labor the football business a little bit further, the Haverhill Weekend—specifically the *fun* of it—was an agreeable contrast to our season's opener at St. Ives, in which play got rough, tempers ruffled, and sportsmanship poor. Such circumstances often bring out the worst in spectator behavior, and in this case that happened. It is futile to try to assign fault. What was clear was that both sides—players and supporters—behaved badly. I am glad to say that the Seven Schools Association has taken steps to address the ancient issue of sportsmanship, and there is a real commitment on behalf of the member schools to stay mindful of our stated priorities in athletics.

There has, of course, been more than studies and sports this fall at Wells. *Ted Burgermeister's* Underformer Players gave us a crisp and hilarious *Mikado* the week before Thanksgiving, and the Dramatis Personae, also under Ted's direction, will stage Eliot's verse masterpiece, *Murder in the Cathedral* in Perry Chapel the week before Christmas Recess.

Recent alumnus *Calvin Kingery* returned for a special

Long Assembly with the Yale *Boolas,* in which Calvin sings baritone and is responsible for a good deal of patter between songs. Students gave them a rapturous ovation for a deceptively casual, well-sung, decidedly racy program. "Sweetheart of Sigma Chi" was not sung. In what may sound in a more highbrow line, but which actually wasn't, the *Rev. Clive Clague,* Rector of St. Christopher's Church in Middlebury Center, gave us a slide show and lecture on the meaning of Gothic in the Middle Ages. Not only was the talk itself a popular success, our art cottage has since been virtually churning out stained glass, Carolingian calligraphy, ceramic gargoyles, ewers, and lank, angular statuary: a Gothic revival at Wells? We were also given an informative and thoroughgoing introduction to African politics by *Professor Josef Ambioto* of the National Institute, Malawi, and visiting professor in politics at the University of Connecticut.

We have imparted some culture as well this term. *Severance Leach* and the Wells Octet took a program of madrigals to over a dozen public and private schools in New England. They were reportedly received most warmly at some school—name escapes me—in Farmington, and have been asked back. Those of you who subscribe to *Harper's* may have noticed in the October issue that one of the contributors had a Wellsian ring to his name. That was *Phelps Perry III,* a fifth former whose essay, "Still Prep in the Eighties," was a tart, penetrating view of independent-school life as he sees it. No school's name is mentioned, but a reference or two struck resonant chords on this campus. It is, incidentally, a fine article: beautifully written, generous, critical, but by no means trivial. Its concluding lines suggest that, on balance, the private school "can still open doors in the precious 'old tie' (and increasingly 'old skirt') sense, but it can also open doors into real scholarship, ideas, literature, and the arts. Privilege may still buy this boost, but it is undeniably a boost." Highly recommended.

I would like to conclude with another excerpt of student writing. The author (name withheld) is a member of the

Third Form Basic Composition section. From an in-class composition in September, titled "First Impressions of Wells":

> *From the time you wake up and have breakfast in Hall and go to classes and then to lunch, and if you happen to play sports, you don't even get to think about what your doing until dorm study when the only thing left is bed. The work is hard, but this is good. The problem is everybody rushes around from this thing to that like they knew what they were doing. Not me yet.*

Me neither.

Faithfully,

John Greeve

24 November

Mr. Jake Levin
R.D. 3
Petersfield, New Hampshire

Dear Jake,

I'm late getting back to you, not because of a crush of work—there's a little of that, dispatched now, I think—but because of the damned poetry. Truth of the matter is, I can't finish that cancer piece. It's not because of the symbolic "heaviness" of doing so, either (to finish it would be to bring it to death, thus bringing Meg, its inspiration, to death, etc.) It's not that. It's that I don't have anything more inspired to say about it. Some of the images of being ill and hopeless from the inside may be arresting in a morbid sort of way, but they are not on their way to *meaning* anything. It seems to me that the only poems that work are those whose meaning comes straight out at you. They are "overdetermined" like Freud's dreams. The good bits, the lucky images, etc., participate in the larger meaning. In that way too, I suppose, good poems, like dreams, are generated unconsciously, in the sense that they aren't consciously worked out or planned as wholes. This isn't to say that the writer of a great poem is not conscious of what he is doing; I happen to think that he is and that *he,* his personality, is responsible in large part for the results. The poem—the meaning—comes out of the poet's deepest knowing, but the poetics, within the limits of his training and reading, are largely a matter of luck, with better devices tending to attach themselves to better themes.

Anyway, my cancer poem doesn't have a meaning or a theme—and themelessness isn't a theme, although I'll bet you've taught many a bearded seminarist that it is. A pack of images organized around a voice do not a poem make, although this formula seems to cover *every* contemporary poem in every journal, except the Catholic ones, that I have read in the past ten years. Agree? We don't get themes any more in poems, we get voices. And since most voices, even tarted up with odd punctuation, surrealist imagery, and curious arrangements of print, aren't very interesting, there has been a premium on spooky voices. I suppose this is why practically every poem in the *New Yorker* or *Poetry* is in the present tense (in the *New Yorker* even the stories are in the present tense) and very likely in the *second person,* a hopelessly illogical and irritating device—

> *You wake to fog but there is*
> *no fog you move to a mirror and*
> *it is a window and through its fog*
> *you see clearly*
> *a light in a window*
> *framing a man*
> *standing at his mirror*
> *lost in fog*

Admit it. Admit that it is no better or worse than practically everything you have read in "little magazines" this year. It is not only bad, it's derivative. Robert Service was less derivative. There's a moral dimension to it, too. All this standing about, being a "voice," reporting surreal nonsense or, worse, reporting the commonplace as if through the eyes of a dinosaur—

> *Her fingers alight on a pale ovoid,*
> *Extract it from its half-hole.*
> *It is cool on the pads of her fingers,*
> *on her palm. Against black iron rim*
> *She half-drops, half-holds it*
> *Running, escaping now from its center,*
> *She widens it, releasing a viscous pool*
> *About an orange-gold sun,*
> *Becoming, yet no longer, egg.*

Fascinating stuff. Morally, if all this voicing and dumb gaping is taken seriously, it amounts to a kind of pantheistic tolerance of anything. I read a prize-winning poem this month about the clubbing to death of a dog—no esthetic or ethical framework, no canine "Out, Out—", just a starkly rendered, highly specific animal mauling. Contemporary art. Onto which heap I don't care to throw my impressionistic pastiche of images about having a debilitating disease. There is of course a theme, a point to cancer, not only to cancer itself but to every particular cancer. But I don't happen to know what it is, haven't the courage or the intelligence to know, or whatever it takes. No poem in that, which isn't to say I couldn't win a prize.

I would like to know what poems you *need*. What do you, in your heart of hearts, go to for nourishment? I want the truth. The poem I have read with the deepest satisfaction this year is Arnold's "Thyrsis." It is about resurrection and striving and hope. He believes in them. He half has it and teases you in after him. You must agree that if those themes are dead, we are dead—yet nobody is writing them. Too hard, I suppose, too big a risk. And no prizes.

Forgive the grousing. I feel I'm doing more of it these

days. The headmaster is a crank and a reactionary. I am actually, strange to say, a little stir crazy. The boys have been gone for four days and won't return till Sunday PM. I've been in the study—crackling fire, brandy, dozing, desk work of a not too taxing kind—usually just my kind of thing, but I'm finding it eerily unsatisfying. Outside the study is another world, quite divorced from mine, a uniformed little system orbiting around Meg. It covers front hall, kitchen, laundry, stairs, landing, upstairs sitting room, and master bedroom (Meg's). Anywhere outside that beaten path is all mine. It is strange that Meg's nurses and Meg seem to belong legitimately in the house, but I, for some reason, feel like a trespasser, sometimes even a shade, as I pad around in slippers, embarrassed to meet a nurse. Going out is worse, though. In a fit of laziness, I went out to lunch, to a popular restaurant hereabouts which features crêpes of all sorts (crêpes rhymes with grapes in our region). Terrible experience. I didn't know where to look. Never go to a restaurant alone without something fascinating to read.

Meg and I passed a quiet Thanksgiving together, both of us trying not to swell up with confusing feelings about Brian and extended family, with whom we normally spend our holidays. The fact of Meg's cancer is by now so pervasive that it has lost any power to frighten us. We can talk about it almost the way we can about inflation. In all, we have about an hour of concentrated conversation every day, perhaps a half hour at the longest single stretch. We talk about topical things, my news from school or the papers, hers from the nurses or from television. So sharp is Meg's intellectual acumen that she can derive amusement and generate good talk from watching television. I hate it in the abstract, but it has been a godsend for her. It is marvelous how her naturally literary approach to life transforms what she watches. Since nobody on those stifling daytime serials or on the talk shows seems to be credibly connected to a world of work or to flesh-and-blood companions off camera, Meg is able to speculate hilariously about what the physicians in the serials would be like in a consultation with, say, Arnold Lieber, the school's maintenance director, or how they might work alongside one of our household nurses. It is her feeling, based on fairly close viewing, that Johnny Carson is not nice. She notes how, when a guest is boring the audience and him, he mugs in that well-known way of his, but there is also a real, icey cruelty in his eyes. She finds him "lupine." I admit to coming around to her point of view after watching him for a while in her company. He certainly couldn't maintain his stiffly jocular approach to life off the camera; the strain would kill him. He is undoubtedly cruel and lupine, if only to relax.

I was about to say that TV was not getting to the essential Meg or to me, but in reviewing that last paragraph, it is very clear that both of us have been deeply affected.

We have heard nothing from Brian, and if I don't hear something this week, I am going to step up my worrying. He has never failed to greet us in some fashion on a major holiday. It is hard on Meg to imagine dying without ever seeing him again, although I personally dread more conveying to Meg that something awful, including the worst, has happened to Brian.

But enough of that. How's tricks in the woods? Did you shoot your own turkey, or is that no longer ecological? I meant it about wanting to know your reading. I am not searching your soul or measuring your taste. I am out for nourishment myself. I dearly hope *Eve of St. Agnes* passes its annual test later this evening.

A nurse calls—most unusual. I must go.

Best,

John

28 November

Mr. Francis Laughlin
Poetry Editor
Commonweal
232 Madison Avenue
New York, New York

Dear Mr. Laughlin,

I am submitting the enclosed poem for your consideration for *Commonweal*.

I am not sure if you require much personal background from those who submit unsolicited material, but for what it's worth, I am a schoolmaster who has published some poems and some criticism and some reviews in "little magazines" and in professional journals.

Because the enclosed has a living referent, I wonder, in the event that you decide to print it, if I might use a pseudonym? If so, "J.G. Oberon."

My good wishes,

John Oberon Greeve

THE DEAD BURY THEIR DEAD

Here lies a woman dying,
One thing, then another, is taken away,
And she becomes the knowledge of her disease,
An apple feeling where its worm has been.

The presence of this process
We solemnly attend,
Repeating until our worry wilts
A story about ending.

A story about ending,
Death: a dream we dream to deny
The itch, the bursting, the bloom,
The apple, the eating, the worm.

Mr. Terrence Doherty
1745 Woodrow Drive
Bryn Mawr, Pennsylvania

Dear Terry,

I received your thoughtful letter and your resumé this morning, and I am writing at once to say I find both very impressive. There is not, however, a position open or, so far as I can see ahead, one opening up in social studies. There may well be a position in math, but that is hardly up your street, is it? At any rate, school personnel, especially these days, have a way of surprising one, so the outlook may be altogether different in the spring, which is when contracts are offered and when most hiring seems to be done. Consider yourself applied.

One caution, however—and pardon me if this is something you have already thought through. There is a certain lure for one about to begin teaching to return to alma mater. This is sometimes, but not always, a good thing. Because, for better or worse, Wells is familiar ground for you, it may be a little too easy to imagine. The whole terror and glory of beginning to teach, it seems to me, involves making exertions and adjustments you never imagined. For this reason, even if you would like to work at Wells ultimately, it might be a fine thing to cut your teeth on another school, perhaps a very different kind of school, for a couple of years.

Believe me, Terry, I value very much the kind words about the quality of your experience here. I hope you know how mutual the feeling is. It is good to be in touch.

If you don't mind, I'll pass the prospect of your candidacy, with resumé, around to my fellow heads in Seven Schools and keep an eye out for openings elsewhere in New England. Please convey my warmest regards to your mother and father.

Faithfully,

John Greeve

REMARKS TO THE SCHOOL

Welcome back. You look to me well-fed and rested—at least you boys do. The faculty, if you'll observe closely, looks pale and wan. I am sure this is due to their feverish grading of your exams. Believe me, taking them for four or five hours bears no relation to the tedium and stress of grading them for forty. It's a wonder we do it. Incidentally, for those of you changing classes or sections this term, do collect your exams and other first-term work today, if possible. Today, remember, is the first day of the winter term, not the last day of the fall term.

It's important to make each day count, considering that there are only 19 shopping days and 17 school days till Christmas. This odd, inconvenient wedge of time between Thanksgiving and Christmas is always, for some reason, the best time of the year. I don't quite know why that is so.

The most obvious answer is that it resonates with old, cosy childhood associations with the holidays, visions of free time, skiing, and loot. But it is more than that, because actual school life is fun, too. It might have something to do with the opening of winter sports: the *first* basketball game, wrestling and swim meets. And the upper form play is always somehow especially galvanizing for falling when it does. At least one good, authoritative snowfall usually helps, too. There is of course our last night's Candle Sing, but that's just the capstone, the *recognition* of what feels so good. I'd like to think the spirit comes a little from the Christmas drives, from that glorious theme of giving things away that is so hard to summon up during the other months. Whatever it is, it's wonderful, and I hope that each of you can find a way to play a part in it.

On a more somber note: Seniors! Contrary to all pernicious rumor and false tradition, the academic year is not over. College admissions officers do *not* read all but the last two columns of your transcripts. Do not slump. I repeat, do not. No matter how far you think you have come, no matter how great the sophistication, it is as easy as sloth to turn stupid again overnight, just as in some sort of academic fairy tale. I have personally seen it happen hundreds of times. So be warned, seniors—models, leaders, examples to others, etc.

And to the rest of you, good morning.

2 December

MEMO to Arnold Lieber
Maintenance

Arnold,

I am afraid it is time for the Christmas tree again. This year, for a novelty, let's not make war about this. We need a full-sized, at least 15′ spruce for the commons. The boys will trim if you and Andy will haul out the ornaments. Please do not ask me about aluminum trees, and please do not remind me of how many aluminum trees we could have purchased for the price of the last dozen real ones. We could save even more if we put up no tree. In my opinion, an aluminum tree is not a tree. They don't smell right.

Merry Christmas,

J.O.G.

3 December

Ms. Camilla Lang
Editor, The Home Forum Page
The Christian Science Monitor
1 Norway Street
Boston, Massachusetts

Dear Ms. Lang,

I enclose for your consideration, I hope not too late, a short Christmas poem.

I am not sure if you require background information from those who submit unsolicited material, but, for whatever interest it may provide, I am a schoolmaster who has written occasional poems, essays, and reviews for magazines.

My good wishes,

John O. Greeve

THIS CHRISTMAS

For it to be true,
And for us to know it,
Wouldn't it occur in the cold,
In a near absence of light,
Eclipsed, perhaps, by a festival
Of carols and all our gaudy hopes—
Like this?

---

4 December

Mr. William G. Truax
President, Fiduciary Trust Company
P.O. Box 121
New Haven, Connecticut

Dear Bill,

Thanks for your prompt and frank appraisal of my "Wells: Ten Years..." draft. I am sorry it did not appeal, but I guess I knew it wouldn't.

I am afraid the problem—or maybe my problem—lies in the nature of the assignment. You and the board would like those of us in the ranks to look to the immediate and long-range future of the school and to imagine, when all is said and done, what we would like to *buy*. What you want, at its nub, is a guideline for raising money. Right?

Well, Bill, you know what to raise money for, and you've always known it: faculty salaries, scholarships, maintenance of facilities, and expansion of facilities. A comfortable retirement plan would make a hit. More books in the library is more desirable than otherwise. An enclosed practice space would be dandy. Enough scholarship money to enable us to admit boys according to sheer merit and personal promise would be a dream. I don't think we need a formal plan to make these obvious points. Our predecessors managed to build up quite a coherent and effective Wells without, to my knowledge, the aid of a formal plan. I am serious about that futurist fallacy I wrote you about. There are no *future* criteria on which to shape the future; all criteria are in the past and the present.

I know I sent you "rhetoric," and maybe it needs revising or even scrapping, but it does cover what Wells is up to and what it will be up to in the future—unless it ceases to be a school. What do you mean by "hard data"? *Questionnaires?* Would you really like to know what percentage of the parents or faculty or students preferred improvement to plant over an increased remuneration for staff or increased financial aid? Which preference would be right?

Do you make long-range plans at the bank? What are they based on, expert forecasts of the economy?

We can do better than that because, unlike the economy, which is an amoral aggregate of individual choices about where to lay down money, school is directed by unchanging moral imperatives. School is always in the business of passing on the best of the culture to emerging new members. It is always preserving what is established and testing what is new and promising. The process requires adults who know both about the culture and how children learn. The process requires space and facilities. Up to a limited point, money buys better people and better facilities; beyond that point, there are only marginal improvements and often diminishing returns. Wells, through the largesse of its past boards and alumni, is pretty damned near the point. And I hope we are in the same relative position in a hundred years.

So what's next? For starters, I'll pare down my rhetoric. Then how about my submitting a weighted ranking of capital expenditures necessary before the decade is out, then a similar list of expenditures desired? Would those data be "hard" enough? In the old days didn't people give and bequeath money to schools out of simple gratitude and affection? Or was there some hard data back then of which I am unaware?

I shall revise and resubmit tirelessly until you are well pleased.

With humble obedience,

John

5 December

REMARKS TO THE SCHOOL

I must precede these luncheon announcements with some very sad news. As some of you may already have heard, this morning during the third class, there was an accident in the pool, in which a fourth former, David Lewandowski, was killed. This is still such a surprise and shock to us that it is hard to tell you much about it. Three boys, including one with Senior Lifesaving, decided to take a swim through the midmorning break. David, while swimming in the diving end, may have had a convulsion. Whatever happened, his friends were unable to take hold of him in the water, and by the time Mr. Kreble was called to the scene, David was unconscious. Mr. Kreble and Doug Froehling applied resuscitation techniques until an ambulance arrived, which took David to Three Counties Clinic, where he was pronounced dead on arrival.

I have just talked to both Mr. and Mrs. Lewandowski, who are on their way to school and should arrive early this evening. Those of you who knew David may want to talk with them after dinner. I know that would be an immeasurable comfort to them. Right now they are simply numb with hurt and loss.

Tomorrow morning's chapel will be a formal one in David's memory. The goal for the time being is to do all we can to support David's friends here and the Lewandowskis.

DEPOSITION
To Wells Village Police Department
Wells, Connecticut

This morning, December 5, shortly after the beginning of the third class (approximately 10:05 a.m.) three boys, David Lewandowski, Doug Froehling, and Mark Tepler, were dismissed from their geometry class for causing some sort of disturbance in the classroom. They were not told to report anywhere in particular, and, since school break follows third class, they felt they would have time for a swim. Free swimming in the pool is permitted if an athletic department member approves and if one of the swimmers has passed Senior Lifesaving. In this case, Froehling has passed Senior Lifesaving. When the boys arrived in the pool office complex, Mr. Kreble, who usually gives the permissions, was out. The boys claim some confusion about permission being necessary. They cited other times they had been swimming without faculty supervision or permission and presumed it was allowed.

At approximately 10:25, as the boys report it, Froehling was swimming laps in one of the racing lanes in the shallow end, Tepler was sitting on the pool edge of the deep end, and Lewandowski was diving off the low board. As Lewandowski surfaced from one of his dives, he began thrashing about in the water. Tepler noticed this first, but paid little attention, as he assumed it was only energetic fooling around. When the thrashing persisted for what Tepler estimates might have been a minute or two, he began shouting to Lewandowski asking if he were all right. Lewandowski was by this time "out of control," in Tepler's opinion, and was periodically going under. Tepler, who is not a strong swimmer, swam out to Lewandowski and tried to hook his arm around Lewandowski's waist and haul him to the side of the pool. At this, Tepler said, Lewandowski locked an arm around Tepler's neck and pulled him under. Tepler managed to get free and shouted to Froehling, a strong swimmer, to help. Froehling did not hear the shouts at first, but after a short delay made his way to the deep end and tried to fasten an arm under Lewandowski's chin so as to drag him backwards to safety. At this Lewandowski pitched over and, as with Tepler, the movement forced Froehling under. As Froehling attempted to work himself back up to the surface, he caught an elbow on the side of one eye and was momentarily dazed. Deciding he could not bring Lewandowski immediately to safety, he told Tepler to find Jack Kreble and a rope or a ladder or a pole.

Tepler thinks it may have been a little after 10:30 when he ran from the pool to find Kreble. Froehling meanwhile made repeated dives below Lewandowski and attempted to boost him up to the surface so he could breathe. Feeling this was futile, he swam to the side, got out, and picked up a long wooden bench from against a wall and placed it in the pool. This he used as a prod to nudge Lewandowski into the shallow racing lanes.

At this point, about 10:35, Kreble entered with Tepler. Kreble entered the water and they were able to remove Lewandowski, who was now unconscious, without difficulty. Feeling a pulse, but detecting no respiration, Froehling and Kreble began to apply two-man cardiopulmonary resuscitation. At this point they realized that Lewandowski had swallowed his tongue. They had some difficulty opening his jaw to correct this and, after that, further difficulties in extricating the tongue. When this had been done, cardiopulmonary resuscitation was resumed until an ambulance arrived, a few minutes after 11:00, to take the boy to Three Counties Clinic. At 11:30 we were called and notified that the boy had not revived and was dead on arrival.

The school had been made aware by the boy's parents that he had been taking anti-seizure medication daily as a precaution against the recurrence of a single seizure his parents reported during the past summer. His teachers, dormitory master, and his coaches were all aware of the boy's condition. Both the boy's physician and our resident physician had advised against contact sports, but had allowed others under appropriate supervision. There had been no other evidence of a seizure this fall or winter. Tepler, who is one of Lewandowski's roommates, said Lewandowski had told him about his medication and had told him once that he really didn't need to take it. In light of the date of the boy's most recent prescription, the number of pills remaining in the prescription bottle suggests he probably did not take the medication regularly.

I have had a chance to question the boy's other roommate and his teachers intensively and am convinced that no other drug or substance had been taken by Lewandowski prior to the accident.

John O. Greeve 12/5/19—

6 December

REMARKS TO THE SCHOOL
In Memoriam, David Lewandowski

Boys, ladies and gentlemen of the faculty, Mr. and Mrs. Lewandowski:

It is too soon and too sad to try to put yesterday's tragedy into perspective. What we feel now is a numbing sense of loss. There is undoubtedly some great scheme into which the death by drowning of an able, energetic, sixteen-year-old boy fits, but if so, it is a design perhaps far too magnificent and terrifying for us to comprehend.

What we must all work to keep in mind is that our grief and dread today are not for David but for ourselves. David's fear and discomfort were brief and are now past. Ours, especially today, continues. A death among us, especially of one so young, makes us question bitterly the loss of so much promise. Anyone who knew David Lewandowski knows that his promise was considerable. The deeper dread, though, is of the loss of our own promise and vitality; we have had a stark reminder that our own are not infinite, nor guaranteed, nor safe. David's fatality confirms our mortality, and we don't really want the news.

Difficult as it is, we have got to avert our musings from his fatality to his vitality, for it is in this, not in his passing, that David had something to teach us. Consider David for a moment. He was a new fourth former this year, but there was not, I'll wager, a boy in his form who didn't know him *well* by Thanksgiving. Rarely does a boy take to Wells—and Wells to a new boy—so quickly and so surely. As one housemaster in Hallowell put it, "He was so easy to like." Easy because he was so indomitably high-spirited. No one who has spoken of him to me in the last twenty-four hours has done so without remarking on his laughter, how quickly it would come, how infectious it was, how it was always occasioned by the unexpected or by the lunacy of school life, never, apparently, by the shortcomings of others or at their expense.

David was also a risk-taker, a volunteer. On the campus twenty-four hours this past September, he volunteered to become varsity football manager. He did this because he wanted to help out and because he wanted desperately to be close to football. It is characteristic of him that practically none of you was aware that he was forbidden, on doctor's orders, to play contact sports. His name also appears, I notice, first among the fourth-form volunteers for the Christmas food and clothing drive. He was not yet, as it happens, a first-rate student—in fact, was a little daunted by Wells the first term. But he was not one to let a set-back get him down. Mr. Shire tells me he requested tutors on his own and was in the process of finding his feet scholastically. I am certain he would have done so. His kind always do.

So, in Auden's words, "What instruments we have agree": David Lewandowski was a good boy. And what we came to know this fall, the Lewandowskis have known for much longer. David did, and does, them glorious credit as parents.

106

It is for them, as well as for ourselves, that we so
wholeheartedly appreciate and honor David here this
morning. Mr. and Mrs. Lewandowski, to you go all our
love and support. We cannot lighten your grief, only share
it. We must acknowledge together that this grief could
not have been had David not been the boy he was. Let's
remember and honor that.

Thank you, and good morning.

6 December

Mrs. Florence Armbruster
Mathematics

Florence,

I must ask that with respect to future disciplinary
measures you observe the following policy without fail: if
you dismiss a boy from class for misconduct, make sure he
reports somewhere, either to me or to Phil Upjohn. We are
both well used to receiving such miscreants. If you wish
to do the follow-up yourself, ask the boy to wait in our
offices until you are free. In the event that either of us is
otherwise occupied, Marge Pearse will know what to do
with the offender.

This is *by no means* a suggestion that you have been
negligent or are in some way responsible for the Lewandowski boy's accident. There is no blame to assign there.

I would appreciate your cooperation on the disciplinary
matter. The wrong kind of boy finds it a treat to be
dismissed early from class if there are no other consequences beyond the dismissal. Thanks.

J.O.G.

Mr. and Mrs. Frank Greeve
14 Bingham Drive
Tarrytown, New York

Dear Val and Frank,

This is not a Christmas card. I regret to say it is the opposite of a Christmas card. "He who has the steerage of my course" has for some reason determined to wreck what is traditionally the most lovely passage of the school year, the between-holidays month, when the illusion of good will and anticipated comfort hangs cosily over the old quad like weather. Advent.

Not so this year, I'm afraid. Meg was taken back to the clinic today by ambulance after a night of terrible pain and, late this morning, a very bad hemorrhage. I can't even think about it. She is so miserable and tired and so angry. What an affront this disease is. I am thoroughly convinced that, almost from the time it was diagnosed, this cancer's treatment has served only to aggravate it; cancer may have been prolonged, but Meg has not been. Until now, except for one afternoon years ago on a cruise, I have never seen Meg nauseated the way these drugs have nauseated her. Not until this have I ever seen Meg close herself to others—out of sheer exhaustion, embarrassment, and pain. Meg could never stand to be such bad company as she feels this disease and its "treatment" have made her. Meg was not made to lose her hair and her appetite and her color. She wants to die but rails at the cowardliness of doing it herself. She is not likely to live past Christmas, and I hope to God she is spared the hell of another bout like last night's.

I can't get it into words, but something is so wrong with all of this. It's not the dying or even the cancer—it's the treatment, or the illusion of treatment. Hurtful and terrifying as it is, Meg's dying ought to be in the same run of phenomena as birth, marriage, and parenting. I don't know. This hasn't been right for Meg. It's not the way she should leave us.

108

I'm very full of death. A boy drowned in the pool this week—a terrible wild card, nobody's fault. He seems to have been a borderline epileptic who had gotten negligent with his daily medication and convulsed in the water. A very nice boy, game, very kind, a not-too-bright innocent. The blow to the parents was indescribable, their dignity in the face of it even more so. We put together a quick memorial chapel for them here the morning after. The boys rose to the occasion and to the parents' need like angels. I've never seen anything quite like it, the parents desperately attaching all their parental affection to each boy they got to know. They decided to bury him here and stayed on the campus three days. Going home without him was the hard thing, the real thing.

We have heard nothing from or about Brian, and Meg is now unable to talk about him. I don't know if she thinks about him. I hope not. I don't know myself anymore what I expect or what I want from him. I spend hours at a time, at my desk or lying in bed, when I positively, murderously hate him. Perhaps this has always been there, perhaps the real cause of all that's gone wrong. I don't want to believe this, and for the most part I really don't, but it's a possibility. And if it's true, if that kind of hate is really running my engine, then all this other business, the avuncular reasonableness, the old-shoe headmasterly patter I do, this affection I think I feel for practically all of these boys who have been milling around me for the past thirty-two years—it's all a veil over something pretty ugly.

I've gone over Brian's growing up a thousand times in the last few years. It's all there in bold strokes: only son of headmaster, like son of clergyman, finds adult expectations impossible, so end-runs or self-destructs or compulsively fails. Until his teens, though, Brian wasn't anything more alarming than a little passive and occasionally stubborn. I always think of Brian's and Hugh's respective approaches to performance, whether musical, athletic, or scholastic. Brian would be pleased to master a tune on the piano—would get it note-for-note perfect through solitary practice. Then, when asked to perform, even if only for Meg and me, he would decline. I once begged him to play for company until he wept. Hugh, on the other hand, liked to perform. He was never a show-off, but he always seemed delighted that you would actually like to see or hear something he had been working on. I will never forget one summer evening at Little House when Hugh had haltingly pounded his way through "Bumble Boogie" and we all cheered wildly. Late that night it started to rain, and as I was cranking windows shut in Brian's room, he startled me by saying, "Dad, you know I can play it really well." I don't know what I said, probably something like "I'd love to hear it." But both of us understood that was not going to happen.

I think I understand pretty well the dynamics of Brian's relationship to me and Meg. It's called passive-aggression in the psychoanalytic literature. All adolescents do it to an extent. The idea is for the adolescent to get you by not performing and thus spoiling your expectations. It is very hard to respond to. Real love and support sustain the passivity by reinforcing it; anger fuels it. It's also hard to be angry at the passive kid because *he* isn't (consciously) angry, and he is suffering consequences, too: failure, loss of esteem, lack of mastery, lack of recognition. It's deadly. Whole lives are organized on the principle. In my view, though, a lot more kids grew out of it before drugs. Kids always like to frustrate parental ambitions (even Hugh, who is perfect, is not an entrepreneur yet), but they also like to please and to acquire skills—social skills, vocational skills, recreational skills, intellectual acumen—and this requires growing up, knitting onto and using the adult order. Drugs block this healthy transition. They have done it to dozens of boys I have known well, and I believe in my bones they've done it to Brian. Drugs are made for passive-aggression. In the old world, in which we may be the graying last generation, being high (without chemicals) was the reward of achievement: goal reached, girl won, etc. Now being high (with chemicals) replaces achievement, *is* the achievement—no behaviors necessary, no mastery, no exchange of favors with the world.

School has always been an adult-adolescent battleground, but the battle was so much more invigorating and honorable before drugs. We can only, usually, guess if a boy is stoned. Druggy boys can get us every time. They can play their heads like chemical juke boxes, while we are drilling for order, for esthetic response, for logical subtleties. Masses of contemporary young never get very subtle. Their language and discrimination are fuzzed, perhaps a little, perhaps a lot, but forever. Medical schools, businesses (as you know) will accept them: the arts expect them. Which does not prove, at least to me, that drugs are harmless. Consider the medicine we get, consider the manufacturing, marketing, and delivery we get; consider the arts. Take Val to the movies, Frank. Take her to *Apocalypse Now*. Listen to the diction and syntax of talk-show guests—and of the host. I can imagine, without irony, a near future in the West in which the culture can *only* be endured with drugs.

But the hell with the near future. My present is hardly manageable. My near past is what I would like to understand better. I saw Brian grow up sweet, bright, maddeningly private and tentative. But promising! I saw him waver and grow tense at fifteen, and after that I never saw him entirely clear headed again. Which, in our particular Oedipal combat, is just about perfect, since being a clear-headed member of humanity is possibly my only firm expectation of Brian.

I know damned well I'm right about drugs. Historians millennia hence will perhaps cite me in their treaties on the Pax Americana in decline. But I still lose. Passive-aggression and its chemical props beat me easily. Brian has rendered me sad, frustrated, angry, and helpless, has done worse—or is it better?—to his mother. He has shown us and our WASPish liberality to be ineffective, and the only cost was forfeiting a comprehending, connecting life. Twenty years ago, passive-aggressive or not, Brian would have seen this, seen through it and past it.

Don't let these ravings frighten you, either of you. It's good for me to get them out, and it beats lying awake.

Thanks so much for all your support. Am living for your arrival at Christmas. It will be gruesome for you, but I love you for it. Best to Hugh.

John

9 December

Mr. Francis Laughlin
Poetry Editor
Commonweal
232 Madison Avenue
New York, New York

Dear Mr. Laughlin,

I am enclosing another poem for your consideration. It is not terribly seasonal, but perhaps it may work into your scheme of things for the new year.

Faithfully,

John O. Greeve

THE NEW SONS

When all the boys were at last bored
With their fathers' gleaming automobiles,
After they, specters in all their hair,
Smells, grit, and gypsy gear
Had spoiled their mothers' brilliant kitchens,
Knew too much or too little for learning,
Had fallen to drugs or drifting,
When these, shameful in their own soil,
Had ceased sullenly to matter,
There were new sons.

Such boys. Modest but alive
With questions, interested in no machine

Nor manning any, they spoke like sages,
Venerated the good and left the famous
Open-mouthed before the public;
Disease and its massive medicine gave way,
And there was simple health; houses
Came to fit the features of their families;
Between each city a distance restored
And with it wonder.

Mr. and Mrs. Asa Lewandowski
1446 Trelawney Avenue
Rumson, New Jersey

Dear Mr. and Mrs. Lewandowski,

Although so much was said this past week, I want to say once again how completely and thoroughly the thoughts and love of everybody here are with you. While you were here, the services and the talk made David seem very much among us. Now will be the tough time. I am glad your daughters and their families are there for your support.

I have enclosed the copy you requested of my hastily composed remarks for the memorial chapel. They should have been fuller and stronger, but they do suggest something of the affection in which David was held here.

I also enclose David's journal for Mr. Hodge's composition class. David may have told you that the class was required to write at least a page per day on any subject. I think you'll agree that something of David's energy and enthusiasm shine forth from this log—it's David, all right.

I have not forgotten your kind offer of a commencement prize in David's name nor your intention to contribute money set aside for his tuition here to a scholarship candidate. You honor us very much with both gestures.

There is plenty of time to work out the particulars, so please don't bother about them for the time being.

I will convey your regards to Mrs. Greeve.

> With my love and
> good wishes,
>
> John O. Greeve

12 December

Mr. and Mrs. Kenneth Ryder
175 Old Church Road
Dedham, Massachusetts

Dear Mr. and Mrs. Ryder,

By now Carl has told you about his latest trouble here in the biology lab. Frankly, we find ourselves baffled by it. We don't know whether it is an instance of childish cruelty, or submerged anger, or of something else. Carl himself doesn't seem to be sure. The startling fact of the matter is that during Morning Break yesterday, Carl made his way into the lab and proceeded to cut off the tails of our six gerbils. Fortunately, I think, he was spotted by Mr. Fiore leaving the lab some time during mid-break, so we have been spared the unease of wondering who among us mutilated the animals.

The incident raises a number of concerns.

1 • Is Carl a danger to other boys and to property here? We are fully aware that many boys pass through a phase of murderous cruelty to animals. Some boys half-sublimate this into "experiments." Some turn it inward into temporary phobias of mice, spiders, etc. Many let it run its course through hunting, exterminating pond frogs or some other easy prey until the impulse is either dissipated or brought under control. John Steinbeck's *The Red Pony* is very instructive in this regard. Something of this destructive impulse is still obviously at work in Carl. What concerns us most is that he is too old for it. I hope the mortification of being caught doing such a thing becomes a first step in his being able to assess his urge objectively and thus bring it under control.

2 • What will it do to Carl's rather fragile sense of esteem to be known, as I am afraid is already becoming the case, as the boy who cuts tails off gerbils? Such acts, again because they are so unconsciously appealing to emerging adolescents, are not readily forgotten. Cruel/funny labels are often applied, and sometimes they stick long after the event that inspired them is forgotten. Mind you, we do not encourage this, but there is little we can do to prevent it.

3 • Has Carl posed us a disciplinary or a psychological problem? Both, I think, but we are trying to treat it more as the latter. I am convinced by his remorse (copious tears) that he is not proud or pleased about what he did; getting nabbed just may put the lid on that impulse for good.

But we intend to help him seal that lid. Our terms for keeping him on here must be as follows. He should have a psychological evaluation by someone acceptable to you sometime over the Christmas recess. I would like to see a written summary of that evaluation when he returns in January. Beyond that, we would impose no further discipline nor require any kind of therapy, unless that is recommended by his evaluator and you choose to carry on with it. However, should Carl be involved in another incident of cruel behavior to animals or to others here or to himself, we are going to insist that he go through at least one term of schooling away from Wells, during which a regular course of counseling would be required for his readmission. I really do not think that will happen or that such measures will be necessary, but, as I said, their clear statement may help keep that 'lid' on until the developmental pressure is eased.

4 • What to do about the gerbils? This is almost too trivial to mention, but the problem is perplexing. The gerbils, now tail-less, appear to be fine and healthy.

They serve, however, as a visual reminder of what Carl did to them, and this isn't good. On the other hand, they have become special pets of some of the third formers who would be hurt and incensed if they were removed—and would hold Carl accountable for any such action. Be that as it may, my own feeling is to buy six new gerbils, at Carl's expense, I think, and find the others homes in Wells village. This should go best for Carl in the long run. I am afraid there is no way to ease Carl's embarrassment in the coming two weeks, but after Christmas, given boy time-sense, the event will seem remote history.

Please write or call me if I can be of any further assistance or if I can clarify further the conditions I have set down. I think you will agree that they are not harsh; they are, however, firm.

My good wishes
for the holidays,

John O. Greeve

13 December

REMARKS TO THE SCHOOL

I could not bid you on your way this morning without remarking on the exceptional experience I had last night as a member of the opening night audience of *Murder in the Cathedral*. It was not only the finest production of that work I have ever seen—and I have seen three: one at Harvard University, one in England *in* Canterbury Cathedral, and one in New York—it is also the finest schoolboy production of *anything* I believe I have seen. Mr. Burgermeister and players have more than done it again.

I don't know why I so easily forget, but I do, that a well-made play is like a potentially living thing, and when life is breathed into it by convincing acting and by intelligent interpretation, the experience is always richer and more powerful than one can ever imagine outside the theatre. I have also not yet kicked the bad habit of thinking, before the action begins, that I am about to watch a *school* play, rather than just a play. I think last night's performance may have cured me permanently of that. As Plato liked to point out, a perfectly tuned string is tuned regardless of who in particular tunes it; similarly, a play brought to life by bright adolescents is as *done* as a play can be. The Royal Shakespeare Company itself could not have come closer to Mr. Eliot's heart, and through that, to the truth, than our Dramatis Personae did last night.

It has not really been a happy time with us here lately, has it? And I must say that I myself, for a variety of personal reasons, have probably been gloomier than anybody else, but that experience last night of getting vividly in touch with ideas and with meaning—well, that was a tonic.

I will be there again tonight, I've decided, and hope that all of you who have not seen it yet will join me.

Good morning.

13 December

Mr. William G. Truax
P.O. Box 121
New Haven, Connecticut

Dear Bill,

Thanks for your letter and for the copy of the Durham School plan.

I wish, though, that you had at least commented on the substance of the plan, which I presume you have read and of which, I further presume, you approve. I am afraid receiving it makes me feel a little like a dull student who has been given a brighter lad's composition to look over for instruction and inspiration.

The Durham plan is certainly streamlined, and the

"hard data" awesome, but it projects some awfully worrying things. If this plan comes true, Durham is going to be a way station for clusters of all kinds of boys and girls who will go there to "tool up" in Durham "skills mods" and "research mods" for six weeks and then return, tooled, to their own less streamlined schools. Although the plan doesn't say so in so many words, Durham, if they actually do this, proposes to cease being a school and to become instead a "resource center" for the nation's public- and private-school complex. Let me tell you what I think of that. (1) It's rather condescending to other schools which are also, most of the time, engaged in skill-building and research activities themselves. (2) Durham, big and rich as it is, isn't big enough to process through more than a negligible fraction of the public/private-school population they are aiming at. (3) The proposed "mods" are too expensive to attract many students beyond the ones who are already clients of private schools or the poshest public-school districts. (4) Durham will no longer be interesting once it recomposes itself; there will not be a community of scholars, nor a community of teachers. At the base of it all, I think, is that Andy Ames has been embarrassed about heading a powerhouse prep school like Durham ever since he took over. He is a man who did not make his reputation in schools but in something much more grand called Educational Theory. He said so many brave new, anti-elitist things from his throne at Columbia in the sixties that he has got to reconcile his contradictions. I'm all for that, but I don't see why a great (if too big) American school should have to go down the drain for it.

But I am undoubtedly mouthing off for nothing. Perhaps you sent me Durham's plan just to show me what a proper job looks like. It's a hell of a plan, I agree. Ames is a giant among planners. If I had the money, I'd lay him on to ghost a plan for Wells, but I'm afraid a kind of hotel-hospital for burnt-out teachers might result. Better yet, we could become a traditional-school lab, in which everything would be more or less as it is, except various administrators-in-training would come through and practice making innovations. I would prefer this because there would still be a role for me. They could bring me in between innovators to restore torpor and aimlessness.

Bill, I am not being defensive. I don't want you to think that for a minute. I'll plan, I'll plan.

If I may be serious after all that nonsense, I am awfully concerned about the Stone-Wilcox suit. I am even more concerned about Seymour's handling of the matter. According to him, I may have made Wells vulnerable to an unfavorable ruling in a number of ways, but first and foremost by announcing what had happened and who was involved before the faculty and student disciplinary recommendations were made. I cannot believe there is much in this. For one thing, the boys had already admitted to everything I told the school, and they had also told their friends. Moreover, I did not pass a character judgment on any of the boys involved, nor did I indicate what their "sentence" should be. In no way did I depart from the stated or traditional due process of the school or from the disciplinary contract all parents sign, including Mrs. Stone. That contract states, in effect, that expulsions are made at the discretion of the headmaster, who may seek student and faculty counsel as he sees fit. Bill, if Seymour can't win this case hands down, there will be no effective disciplinary process in the future. This is perhaps the neatest and most routine expulsion I can remember.

I wish to make no cash settlements or other substantive compromises out of court. Seymour has led me to believe that Mrs. Stone's principal aim is to correct what she feels has been personal mistreatment of Charles and her: my addressing the whole school about Charles's drug deal and perceived slights in my letter to her. I regret now that I wrote her the same letter I wrote the Wilcoxes, but it pertained adequately, and I was pressed. Seymour says that if I alter the status of the dismissal to a voluntary withdrawal and draft an encouraging letter of recommendation to the colleges of Charles's choice, she might, for lawyers' fees to date, drop the suit. I sense that Seymour likes this, as it will keep Wells and its association with

drugs out of the New York and Boston papers. No mean
consideration, I agree. But wrong. We did right by Charles
and right by Wells in this case, and it's important that we
don't forfeit that gain. Why should Mrs. Stone—for those
motives—get satisfaction? Please support me on this, Bill.
I don't want to see Wells smeared, and I don't want to see
Mrs. S. have the satisfaction of hauling me to court to
defend myself, but the principle is worth it. In fact, I
dread the prospect of court. It couldn't be a worse time for
me, although I understand we are getting delays until
January. After we win the case, or she drops it, I will be
glad to write to Mrs. Stone apologizing for the inadequa-
cies of my letter. I'll also recommend Charles to somebody
some day, if he ever pulls himself together.

Why does so much about school feel like a fight? And
why doesn't it feel like school unless it's a fight?

Thanks for your kind words about Meg. There is too
much for me to say about that right now to say anything.
She is very bad, Bill, and unlikely to make it through the
holidays. My brother and his wife are coming up here for
Christmas, and we are going to hold each other together.
You and Marguerite have been a terrific help. I think you
know how Meg feels about you both.

Have a joyful holiday,

John

14 December

Mrs. Herman Triester
2006 Apple Mountain Road
Williamstown, Massachusetts

Dear Mrs. Triester,

Thank you for your frank and thoughtful comments on
my "Headmaster's Notes" in the *Quarterly*.

I think I may be less guilty of espousing the bad ideas
you attribute to the article than I am of being insufficiently
clear about what I did say. By no means did I want to

suggest that "grade-grubbing" was a welcome development—
for itself—at Wells. I did mean to say that on balance boys
seem willing to work hard again, and there might be
some good in this.

I am no foe of "learning for its own sake," although I
happen to think that term is tossed about a good deal as
an intrinsic educational good, but rarely examined for
meaning. Considered seriously, the notion poses problems.
Learning seems to me to be perfectly instrumental, to be
invariably for the sake of something else: reward, promotion,
amusement, mastery. Different souls learn things for different ends, and some ends are undoubtedly nobler than
others, but learning itself is never the end. An eight-year-
old learns the multiplication tables so as to feel competent at an age-appropriate level, not really out of a desire
to perform the practical tasks that multiplication allows
him to do (which is still instrumental), and certainly not
out of love of arithmetic elegance. We learn those basic
things because we are supposed to, and because we'd be
ashamed not to. And so it goes with the other enabling
skills. Without them, learning, however it was acquired,
would only be what accidentally accrued as one pursued
impulsive desires. Of course there is an educational theory in that, revived from Rousseau and plunked down in
the nineteen sixties, when there was a new population
willing to believe that if you don't block the youthful
learning engine with stultifying conventions, it will run,
run, run to the benefit of the learner and his society. This
has always sounded marvelous, but it's false and the
desired result never happens.

There is an occasional practical genius like Edison who
was genuinely uneducated but who nevertheless synthe-
sized experiences in such a way as to contribute to the
culture, but he is one in a million, perhaps one in ten
million. My own feeling, based on a fairly interested
reading of Edison's life, is that ordinary schooling would
have imposed little on his mechanical aptitude and might
by way of compensation have added some order, perspective,
and appreciation to his badly muddled adult life. Rousseau,

by his own *Confessions,* was worse: the genius of progressive child-rearing gave his own away; he had no time for them. You also mention Da Vinci, who, while incontestably a genius, was hardly unschooled. He had a marvelous humanist education from Florence, just as Socrates had from Athens.

One can't know these things for certain, but let me offer you two basic propositions. (1) Boys who work hard or are made to work hard at acquiring verbal and logical facility at school will be more productive in any endeavor than similar boys who do not. (2) Boys left to their own devices, especially adolescent boys and adolescent devices, seek only gratification of their impulses in the most sensational, yet most effortless, ways possible. Consider any example, historical or contemporary, of adolescents left to their own devices. Adolescents, at least half of them, grow out of adolescence, but if they are unschooled they are crippled in taking up their adult purpose.

Of course I am laboring, and probably blurring my point. In large measure I agree with you. Nobody is more heartened to observe a student "see the point" than a schoolmaster. My experience, however, has taught me that the odds of seeing it are greatly increased when the vision is trained. I don't worry about the self-esteem or the sensitivity or the "creative potential" of any boy working doggedly at school. Hard work brings achievement, which is the only sure source of self-esteem—I say this in spite of the odd psychological theoretics afoot that talk about self-esteem as if it were a wonderful visceral potion, somehow stopped up by pressures to perform and to produce. As for sensitivity and creativity, my experience again is at odds with popularly expressed sentiments. My own view is that sensitivity and creativity from the young are rarely welcomed by anybody. If you are talking about creativity in the sense of feeling and acting like an Alienated Artist—Byron, Shelley, Joyce—then the best bet would be to enroll the prospective artist in a perfect prison of a school, a place with no outlet whatsoever for their finer sensibilities. Seemed to work for Byron, Shelley, and Joyce and for many lesser lights. I would also be intrigued to see a school designed for Byron, Shelley, etc. I think it's possible. I can see, in fact have seen, the curricula that would make every provision for creativity, set aside appropriate modules of time for spontaneity. Ah, give me Tom Brown's Rugby, and I'll give you not only Thomas Hughes, but also Matthew Arnold.

Please forgive this garrulous reply. You have struck my one chord (maybe only a note).

Again, I appreciate your letter, criticism and all. Would you mind if we printed it in the March *Quarterly*?

Best Wishes for
a joyful holiday,

John O. Greeve

15 December

Mr. Brooks Forbes
145 East 79th Street
New York, New York

Dear Brooks,

I am going to begin by attempting what has proved futile in the past, but which is still absolutely necessary if civilized conduct is to prevail at Wells. Will you please, for God's sake, accept this modest honorarium for your travel and for your time? I happen to know that you get less than a full day off per week from the *Strictly Waugh* production, so let us compensate you a little.

Your reading here undid all of us, got under the hide of *every* dullard, tough, and sophisticate. I love it! I love that it worked, and I love that for almost two hours, the Wells hall could have been the schoolroom at Charterhouse or Harrow a hundred fifty years ago, with perhaps Dickens himself doing the honors. I've gotten so used to the Alistair Sim movie, that I forgot how much meat there is in the *Christmas Carol*. Can you imagine having written that, and only that? I was reminded during the various charges up my spinal column which accompanied your reading of what the novelist John Irving said about the *Christmas Carol:* something to the effect that you can't dismiss it as sentimentality when the intensity and resonance of those feelings is the best you've got. Who tried to put us off sentimentality anyway, Freud?

I am like a little boy, Brooks, in that I marvel at the transformation of you in performance. I know you, I taught you, I once slapped you, I introduced you to our boys, and then I took my seat in the Hall and then watched as you evaporated into sheer characters. I am getting that spinal response again just recalling it. Can anything be better than mastering an art as you have and then being able to put it into the service of something sublimely fine as *Christmas Carol*?

Good heavens, this is a fan letter, isn't it? Thanks very much for the guest seats to *Strictly Waugh*. Normally I am in and out of NYC during the Christmas break, but with Meg as unstable as she is, I can't plan on it. How she would love it, by the way.

And, by the way, it was wonderful seeing you—and for the boys to see a living proof that a Wells education does not always lead directly to Philistia.

Do not return the honorarium, or I will write the NY papers and tell them about your balcony scene in *Romeo and Juliet,* spring, 1962.

> Merry Christmas and
> warm wishes,
>
> John

Mr. Charles Pawling
Independent School Services, Incorporated
6 Liberty Square
Boston, Massachusetts

Dear Chet,

I am writing not only to convey season's greetings (season's greetings, Chet) but to make a most unseasonable inquiry about the availability of first-class mathematics teachers who happen to be, for some reason not deleterious of their character, doing absolutely nothing at the moment.

We may be stuck here shortly. We had an annoyingly sudden resignation here late in August and have filled in with somebody who is not working out—decent enough person, though. Anything promising on hand? No hard cases, please.

Best,

John

16 December

Mr. Kurt Kohler
28 Cicada Court
Naples, Florida

Dear Kurt,

Greetings from the north.

I am writing with a proposition so preposterous it may actually appeal to you. How would you like to revive your pedagogical act for a special half-year run at Wells? As the sickly head said to Mr. Chips when the war broke out, "We need you, old man."

The situation is this: a young math appointment (hired since you left) pulled out suddenly in August, and we were left short. I signed on a woman who wanted to get back into the classroom after childrearing, and she is not working out. The school will not collapse if we keep her on for the duration of the year, but a very destructive consensus has been reached by her classes that she is not to be taken seriously. In consequence nearly seventy boys are learning little math, and she is taking a psychological beating.

Of course I have no business intruding into your richly deserved solemnity, but if I can't send an ill-considered appeal to the school's most distinguished, most sagacious, most beloved emeritus master, to whom can I send one?

Seriously, Kurt, if the idea for some reason appeals, let me know. Needless to say, we will pay you bushels and arrange commodious housing wherever you would like. Even if you have no interest in the proposal, why not pretend you do, so that we may fly you up here at our expense and "interview" you? Needless to say, that would positively *make* this academic year.

My good wishes,

John

16 December

Mr. and Mrs. Frank Greeve
14 Bingham Drive
Tarrytown, New York

Dear Val and Frank,

Just a note to let you know I am counting the days till you arrive. Some order at last! Some company I can relax in, at last! I am *hiring* two women from the dorm staff to do our house before you arrive. So if not exactly commodious, it will be damned clean.

I've tried to keep you informed about Meg, but be prepared. She looks much more ravaged than when you saw her before Thanksgiving. If it works out, you should see her, but it will hurt. It will also hurt her, for the same reason. All we can do now is love her. That gets through, I think, although the pain now is constant. If she goes before you leave, I'll call you at once, as that might entail a change of plans on all our parts. It's hard to say much more about that now. Also, no matter how terrible you think *I* look, don't tell me. I'm getting a complex.

This will be an unusual holiday for us, and I am ashamed at how selfishly I want you here, knowing you will not have the serene break from routine that you enjoy so much and that you deserve. Please tell Hugh that he is not obligated to stay an hour longer than he likes. There is a girl in Boston, isn't there?

Love to you all. Drive carefully.

John

17 December

Mr. Jake Levin
R.D. 3
Petersfield, New Hampshire

Dear Jake,

Season's greetings.

I saw your poems in this month's *Poetry*—seemed to be about half the magazine. Very impressive. I had the impression that they were much airier than anything else of yours I've seen. I remember Ruskin rhapsodizing somewhere about the experience of watching—really watching—clouds as they tuft up, leave misty veils, and by almost imperceptible stages re-arrange themselves into new forms. Is this what you're up to? Showing what we commonly perceive as enduring and substantial to be fluid and insubstantial? I hope so, or I shall feel terribly stupid.

By the way, I was glad for your warm letter. Even though people here could not be kinder or more solicitous, they are responding, I suppose quite naturally, to a sad process going on out at the clinic; you, on the other hand, are kind enough to respond directly to me. I need that, I won't deny it.

Meg will probably not live another two weeks, and unless she can be made more comfortable, I hope she doesn't. This has been awful, all of it. To see her so physically diminished is painful, but the horror of this thing is to see her so constantly on edge. She gets no rest or relief from pain, except for a brief hour or so after injections. Riding the nausea and pain requires all her energy. Conversation can no longer divert her. I doubt that you have seen Meg cry and probably have a hard time imagining her doing so. She cries much of the day. It's the inability to rest, I think, more than anything else, and a rage at the unfairness of it.

You go through these things, you know, like a zombie. There are visiting hours at the clinic, and I am there. There is the daily liturgy of school life, and I am there. School teachers, especially headmasters, have to do a lot of acting, but since Thanksgiving the curtain has rarely fallen. It's bad in a way, since I'm supposed to be helping to *shape* the experience here—the board is even hounding me to do a jazzy future plan. But all I do is preside. Not that anyone is making me. I've been invited to take an indefinite leave, to go south, to do whatever I please—but what would that be? That would be terrifying.

I keep telling myself, as if an external voice, that if I weather this, give Meg my all, keep my hand on the wheel at Wells, do right where I can see it, do not fall too hopelessly behind—that will show my people here, maybe even the boys, something important. When at some point all of *their* props are knocked out from under them and they feel themselves collapsing, they'll recall that it's not supposed to be that way—you're supposed to hang in there the way old Greeve hung in there. I hope this is important, because it's all I'm living for. The voices inside are certainly no help. They cry and give up and assign blame, usually ending up focused murderously on Brian. Interesting that the external voice, the one with no energy, prevails. Maybe it won't prevail, maybe I'll crumple up, but it's still interesting that I want it to prevail—*want* isn't even right: that I know it *ought* to prevail.

You know, in spite of all our jaded worldliness, we really don't—at least I don't—think enough about ending up. I'm fifty-five and until this fall I never really thought about it at all except as a kind of vague, unemotional tableau of being white-haired and more decrepit. Seeing Meg has taught me that it's not going to be that way. It's bound to be something very different, probably something I never imagined. With Meg gone, I will no longer be able to be anxious about being cut down prematurely.

Although, with the event at hand, I am still not ready for Meg and me to be over. That is what I never imagined. I have never gotten used to Meg, never lost interest in her for a second. My intellectual superior, my arbiter, my planner, my renewer. After the initial five years with Meg for a confidante, I can honestly say I never again felt inadequate—"one down"—in the presence of anybody. I probably should have, but such is Meg's solidity. She is such a fact. Marriage is just as substantial as the Northern Lights or Joy or the four-minute mile. Not everybody gets the experience, but it's real, and those who try to subvert it on intellectual grounds or to sully it by their own infidelities can only be those who never had it. Sad for them, but they do more harm than they could ever imagine. Believe me, Jake, this isn't sentimentality setting in (or if it is, it's a sentimentality of recognition, not a sentimentality of distortion). My present circumstances do not lead me very readily into Browning-like sweetness. What a thing, though, to have loved somebody, in no elaborately qualified sense, for thirty-two years. And been loved back.

Nothing goes the way one expects. I blink to find myself headmaster of a boys' school in a New England village. I am about to become a "widower." I will, in another deceptive wrinkle of time, blink to find myself *emeritus*, with a Wells rocker—where? In a winterized cottage on the Cape? In a home? Last year I still had a boy's view of the Future. I still thought, against all possible evidence, that an elusive Main Event was ahead. I don't know what I thought it would be. A great book, maybe.

I worry about enduring the school year. The archetypal boy never grows up; he cheats and gets caught, loses himself, finds himself, drops out, drowns, thinks chaotically, thinks brilliantly, keeps graduating and then starting over, teasing me somehow back into the game. His energy never flags and he will have no patience when mine does. A soft and pallid Greeve has been imitating himself for four months. A thin but insistent voice tells him what sounds to make and where to go.

But his friend Jake knows better.

I'll let you know about Meg.

Love,

John

18 December

MEMO
To all faculty

Let me stress in print what I mentioned only briefly in our meeting yesterday: please be on hand Friday in the dorms until the last student is packed off for home. Phil Upjohn and I have warded off an avalanche of requests from Boy and Parent for earlier exits, and we have ruthlessly declined them all, claiming that we are far too committed to the academic process to give up even an hour of precious pedagogy. Hawaii, The Bahamas, St. Moritz, home and hearth can just wait. You can imagine what frauds we will seem in their eyes if you yourselves fly the coop early. And again, *use* those final classes—or else those who wish to do so are doomed. Special, warm, seasonal surprises are fine—so are testing and quizzing— but please do not dismiss classes early or altogether.

That said, I hope every one of you has the most renewing, joyful holiday possible. There are no words adequate to express my gratitude for the uncountable kindnesses you have given me since Meg fell ill this fall. And as many of you know, the only thing she has not resigned herself to in her condition is that it has forced her to be separated from all of you.

From both of us, deepest thanks, warmest wishes for the holiday, and our love.

J.O.G.

20 December

REMARKS TO THE SCHOOL

What a pleasure this morning is. Not—or not *just*—because seventeen and one half days of leisure await us in a few hours, but for the morning itself. Even though it is well known that boys of your age resist sentimentality fiercely, it is awfully hard—and awfully silly, really—to resist it today. If you think about it for a minute, you see that it's not the vacation itself that makes the holiday such a magical prospect. It is having been here, many of us exerting ourselves against the grain, that makes a pause so sweet. It came as a powerful but slightly sad revelation to me years ago that loafing, refreshment, and freedom itself are meaningless states of being, except as contrasted to their opposites. Unless we're bound up in those opposite states most of the time, there is no *pleasure* in loafing, being refreshed, and being free. Can you imagine trying to refresh yourself continually? It would drive you frantic.

This morning is also a pleasure because it is very cold, the snow is very fresh and clean, and Wells Chapel, viewed as I viewed it this morning through a lattice of snowy branches and Hallowell House chimney smoke, has been transformed. No matter how much cheap Christmas cards and the other glittering junk of commercial Christmas have tried to trivialize this season, it can't be done. We all know the cliché, yet the real thing is as new and as fine as the panorama just beyond our chapel steps.

This morning is also a pleasure because, although we are all mortified at the sloppiness of admitting it, we share the heightened feelings of this time of year with the people we like most, even with the whole body of this school. The tradition of it feels good. The carols feel good. They even *sound* good. Like the hot cider and the dark and the nearly holy mood of last night's Carol and Candle Hall, Wells—there is no denying it—has been transformed by the season.

And while rest and relaxation, the snow, the cold, and school traditions are all part of the transformation, they are not all of it. There is something else. It is the thing that is planted deepest in our core, the thing we recognize uncritically as children, yet the thing we find ourselves the most anxious to grow out of. I am of course talking about the mystical center of the tradition, the reason for it, the energy behind it. We can't get away from it, no matter how unreligious we may choose to be. Two thousand years ago it happened. A cluster of less-well-established but pious Jews bore witness to the birth of what they say was everything man has always hoped for. They felt that in this birth lay the solution to every woe and an answer to the riddle of being alive. You all know the outline of the event from Sacred Studies and from Western Civ. classes, but the novelty and the oddness of the claims made about Jesus can not be overemphasized. Divinity itself made into human flesh: a staggering concept, except for infants and younger children.

For infants and younger children, the idea of a holy gift who is also a human baby is not a hard concept. Something inside them has always rather felt that way itself. In fact, the Jesus miracle is perfectly continuous with the Santa Claus miracle. It *is* a miracle, you know, before it becomes a pagan custom. The miracle, if you think about it, is this: a magical grandfather from remote reaches, but who is somehow only a man, visits us in a way we can never quite see, except in story and imagination, and he gives us everything we want, even more than we expect. Children, at least the precivilized ones, have no trouble accepting the reality of the Universal Giver. The world seems to them to be that sort of place. Later, most children know differently, but they never really know better.

The miracle part of Christmas, the part about the human giver who never gives out, is not a charming fiction. We take charming fictions lightly, replace them with updated fictions, and ultimately forget them. But we can't seem to forget this fiction. We can project our feelings about it onto certain of its sideshows like a family ski trip or the loot under the tree, but, as some of you have by now realized, while those things are very nice, there's no magic, none of the *original* feeling in them. But there is, I swear there is, some of the original feeling still at large. I know I heard it last night, for minutes at a time, during Carol and Candle, I know I saw it through the branches on the way over here this morning, and if I am not mistaken, there is some of it among us this very minute.

And as I said, it is a pleasure.

Before I send you off to enjoy the rest of it, I want to take just a moment to thank each of you and all of you for the good wishes, cards, gifts, good company, and blessedly good *behavior* that have enabled me and Mrs. Greeve to endure a really trying illness. What a gift to me, while I am on the subject, to be cared for and buoyed up by the very people I am supposed to be caring for. Thank you.

And now, we will close by singing "O Come All Ye Faithful," four verses; third formers departing as we sing the first, fourth as we sing the second, and so on.

A very merry Christmas to all of you.

PART TWO

Mr. and Mrs. Frank Greeve
14 Bingham Drive
Tarrytown, New York

Dear Val and Frank,

I have just given enough thought to answering a thousand and some condolence letters to know that I can't do it. It does nag me, though, that there are so many people I want and need to thank—you two foremost. I can't place a value on the support and love, but I can place a value on the sheer time you have given us and then me since the holidays. That will simply have to stand as a debt. I suspect you were both aware that for a few days after Christmas I seemed to disappear altogether. It is hard to describe that feeling of nothing being substantial, even the loss, even the grief—odd. I remember for some reason the impression that, whereas the day Meg died, a strong drink took me away from the blackening, falling feeling, a few days afterwards a drink seemed to pitch me into it. And there you were, a solace beyond alcohol.

Home is a place where, when you have to go there,
They have to take you in

Exactly right.

You were both right and not right about my coming here. It is too suffused with Meg for comfort, but that is not the main thing wrong. It's also too insubstantial, too not-enough for what I feel and need right now. It is no company at all, and it shoots me full of the fear that there is no company anywhere. (Pitiful, Greeve, pitiful.) And so I'm taking off. I'd like to pop in on Jake Levin, my poet friend, in New Hampshire, and if he can't manage it, I'll go inn-hopping off the beaten path. It's what I should have done in the first place. I know your place would be easiest, but I have got to toughen up, to practice. I'll drop you cards.

School has begun without me—funny feeling. I'm thoroughly relieved not to be doing it because I can't, but I'm also feeling that August feeling that I couldn't possibly manage a school, even teach a class. It's a funny way for a fifty-five-year-old schoolmaster to feel, but I always feel that way after a lay-off. And if the school manages nicely without me—what then? The hell with it. I shall visit inns and read their books: *Good Morning Miss Dove, A Man Called Peter, Lost Weekend,* etc.

It feels good to write you—like having you here. Best love to Hugh. Don't tell him his uncle, the Headmaster, is folding up.

Love,

John

16 January
Little House

Mr. Jake Levin
R.D. 3
Petersfield, New Hampshire

Dear Jake,

I won't say things have settled yet, but there is enough regularity in the blur that I feel I can get in touch. Now that it's over, it's worse than I thought. You feel prodded by shadows, urged on by something vaguely awful.

Coming here doesn't help. The place evokes Meg and then, by a scrap of handwriting or by a half-knitted sleeve, documents her finitude. She keeps dying.

What I really would like to do is to drive up and see you. Is it possible? I mean now. At any rate, I'm clearing out of here in a few days. I'd clear out immediately, but I have accepted a dinner invitation from some nice, retired friends down the lane—how could they ever understand that my presence in their house confirms their luck and their fragile safety?

May I come? I'll call Monday a.m. at the college. If you can't do it, leave word. If you can, see you soon.

Best,

John

18 January
Little House

Mr. William Truax
President, The Fiduciary Trust Company
P.O. Box 121
New Haven, Connecticut

Dear Bill,

I don't have the fuel yet to acknowledge appropriately the enormous amount of help and love extended to Meg and me over the course of our ordeal, so I won't just yet. I hope you will convey to the board, though, that their efforts and their presence over the holiday period were deeply appreciated.

I am grateful, too, for this open-ended leave. Wells will certainly be better for it. It's a funny thing though; it puts me rather on edge.

Between you and me, hiding away out here was not a good idea. The effect is the opposite of relaxing—almost like being hounded by something. I suspect it's truancy guilt of some kind.

Again, deepest thanks. I shall be back in the saddle soon. I'll be in New Hampshire with a friend for a spell, then back down to Wells. Phil Upjohn and Marge Pearse have numbers to call if you need to get in touch.

Warmest regards,

John

18 January
Little House

Mr. Arnold Lieber
Director, Physical Plant
Wells School
Wells, Connecticut

Dear Arnold,

I can't begin at this point to acknowledge the gracious and feeling letters written to me after Meg's death, but I want to respond to yours before any more time passes.

I was deeply moved by what you had to say about Meg and the school. I don't think anyone else has seen as clearly what she did for the place or what she thought about it. You're right—she *was* the practical one. Unfortunately, perhaps, she was also the imaginative one and the diplomatic one. Wells School did not really have a headmaster; it had us.

Again, Arnold, no letter meant more to me than yours. I'm sure you know that you were always a great favorite of Meg's, and she didn't hand out such distinctions lightly.

I'll be leaving here in a couple of days and heading up to see an old friend in New Hampshire. It wasn't a very good idea to come here. Then on through a bit of New Hampshire and Vermont, then back to Wells—I almost wrote "home."

I hope you and Phil Upjohn are getting on. He has numbers, should you need to call me for anything.

Gratefully,

J.O.G.

24 January
Petersfield, New Hampshire

Mr. Philip Upjohn
Director of Studies
Wells School
Wells, Connecticut

Dear Phil,

Just a note to let you know I am leaving Petersfield tomorrow and will be slowly winding my way down to Wells, via New Hampshire and some Vermont inns. I should be back in a week or so—no longer than ten days—and I will call from time to time.

I assume that all is in order, no doubt in rather better order than if I were pottering about at your side. I hope you know, Phil, how deeply grateful I am that you have been kind enough to stand in during this rocky stretch. I only wish that the additional responsibilities could have fallen on a less busy man. They could not have fallen on a better man.

My good wishes,

J.O.G.

Mr. Jake Levin
R.D. 3
Petersfield, New Hampshire

Dear Jake,

Well, I've found one—and not just "one," but *it*. It's a big old much appended-to frame house with creaky passages and stairways going off in every direction. There's a nice sweet sort of smell of pine soap and something harder to pin down: must and, I think, a little rot. There's a ripply-floored sitting room with a fireplace and clusters of odd chairs and sofas and end tables—all satisfyingly deserted, as the skiing is apparently terrible. Mr. Soughan— "call me 'Harry'"—fixes the meals more or less on call. He is concerned that I don't eat much, and even were I hungrier, this would not be easy, as the fare is awfully tired looking when it is set before one in the dining room (laundry to be sorted on an adjacent table), and Harry is none too fastidious in his personal turnout. What could be better? So far I have borrowed three treasures from the sitting-room shelves: *Marjorie Morningstar* (Wouk), *On the Beach* (Chute), and *Sand and Foam* (Gibran). This trilogy, I have found, runs the full gamut of human possibility—earthly striving, earthly mortality, and transcendence. This is a wonderful place, and it is very quiet.

I hope my morose and even lachrymose presence was not too irritating for you. I could tell it was a little irritating. Nobody who is working should ever have to play host to someone who is not. I am afraid my picture of you in Petersfield was way off. I imagined hours of phoneless, reflective time in which you read, or composed, or dreamed into the firelight. How was I to know you worked so hard? I thought the university job was just a formality, a lucrative honor, like certain British crown appointments before modernity. You actually teach and mark papers and receive callers from their jeeps. And, I never bothered to anticipate, you have friends, among them more than one

attractive woman. And you shop at a mall and cut wood
and drive nearly a hundred miles a day. Unsettling for me
to realize you are not a timeless hermit, but a busy,
productive Modern Man, your poems written not by the
brook's gurgle, but by the hum of the university-library
clock. Men are less busy, less modern at Wells school!
Were it not for this enchanting place and for Harry, I
might think the whole world—even its poetry-producing
dimension—had passed me by. Thank God for *Sand and
Foam*, for the eternal verities.

I want to tell you how I found this place, because the
process is important and rare and nobody ever talks
about it. I *willed* my way here, maybe even willed the inn.
Without a guidebook, without a map, I was united, as if
by a kind of spiritual magnetism, with the exact object of
my imagination. I didn't 'find' this inn; I joined it. I'm
with the Jungians here. This inn was simply on my path.
Only once before do I remember having this experience so
vividly. Thirty years ago when I was reading English at
Cambridge, I suddenly found myself preoccupied with
minerals: crystals and gems. An obsession sprang without
warning from my depths. It had also been an obsession
during a phase of my childhood (ages eight till ten).
Anyway, this crystal obsession finally eclipsed all else,
and I remember springing from my chair one day and
taking to the streets, driven in an altogether different
way than I might have been for a sandwich. I, a relative
stranger to England and to the Cambridge streets, wanted
crystals. I stalked purposefully down Bridge Street past
the colleges, past the shops toward the station, then
suddenly turned up a narrow, coal-blackened lane called
Silver Street, composed mostly of the backs of academic
buildings; turned again up a dust-bin-lined alley, through
an iron gate, up onto a loading platform, through two
heavy service doors, down a passage or two—all without
hesitation, all without encountering another soul—opened
a heavy door and found myself in a large gray storeroom
or laboratory. Black tile counters lined the walls; otherwise the room was full of dusty glass display cases—of

bones, of rocks, and of crystals. On the tops of the cases and on the counters were little heaps of rock, and I somehow moved to the piles that were crystals: honey-colored, maple-colored, wine-colored, diamond-white. Some were fine as slivers of frost, others thick and tooled as smokey ice cubes. There I was, immersed in all the crystals I had ever wanted. Then the rest of the setting began to sink in: the dust, the bones, the cold gray stone crystal beds. It was all very clear. The message wasn't about crystals; it was about time. Something older and bigger and more important was getting in touch with me through those Cambridge rocks. I am reminding you, they said, that your business is just the surface skin of something very old and deep. Don't lose touch. It was the same sort of experience as finding this inn. A reminder.

Of what, though? That's the problem. Once I thought it was going to be glorious, a great achievement or discovery, an occasion even for fame. It is not going to be that, the inn reminds me. It might just be sordid. At any rate, I'm feeling a little jumpy, and I am obliged to leave Harry and Franconia House. Plenty more where this came from.

I can't quite bring myself to head straight down to school and to take it all on again, not just yet. On the other hand, every day I stay away, the less possible it seems that I'll ever be able to do it. How would I handle the first thing? Some mother will phone and complain that her son's roommate is unwholesome, and I will come undone. There will be no solution but to withdraw the boy at once. The mother will be astounded at such a suggestion, and I will stammer and apologize and perhaps ask what she thinks is best since she is a mother and knows boys. Soon the word will be out: Greeve's gone funny, can't think straight.

So what does that leave, my poems? They wouldn't go down with the university set, would they? Not airy enough. They might go down with the *Christian Science Monitor* set, though. *The Christian Science Monitor* has bought several poems of mine recently for up to $20 each. But could I sell them a thousand poems a year and make a modest living? No. That would overexpose me to the *Monitor* readership. No more Greeve! they would write the editor.

For the moment the problems of schoolmastering and of poetry writing seem insurmountable. Perhaps a solution will present itself at the next inn.

It was good to see you, Jake. Everything about you and your world seems very substantial. Thanks very much for the company.

Best,

John

1 February
Peacham Place

Mr. Hugh Greeve
Pembroke House
St. Edward's School
Framingham, Massachusetts

Dear Hugh,

Have you ever been to Peacham, Vermont? Well then you really must go. It's like the illustrations for some almost too precious children's book. But it's true. These old houses and this old inn do sag with the snow in a reassuring way, and apple-cheeked men do stack cordwood, and at rosy-blue dusk scarf-swaddled children come home with their sleds and retire into lamplit parlors. If I were one of those children, I would never leave Peacham.

It looks, however, as though I ought to be leaving Peacham pretty soon. It's become February, and I still haven't been to school. You can get permanently behind, you know. It's a sorry state when the headmaster won't come back after vacation.

How are you? What with grieving and all the business of the funeral, I didn't see enough of you at Christmas time. I did value very much your being on hand, knowing full well you deserved and needed a proper release after your first harrowing term at St. Edward's. Thanks, Hugh. You and your family kept me afloat. I think you know how special you were to Meg.

From what I could see of her, your girl—Jill?—looks mighty appealing. And she is very clearly gone on you. Old Uncle John knows these things. Hope you managed to salvage some fun before New Year's.

Ah, Peacham. I have lived in New England more or less my whole life, and I do not take it for granted. It always takes me in, surprises me, breaks my heart. It's so very old—older than the colonials, older than the Indians. I could retire right here. I may well retire right here. A feeble nay vote for the Sun Belt.

> *The woods are lovely, dark and deep*
> *But I have promises to keep*

Promises I had a lot of nerve making.
  Write!

Love,

Uncle John

2 February
Peacham Place

Ms. Lisa Girvin
Poetry Editor
Yankee Magazine
Box 16
Dublin, New Hampshire

Dear Ms. Girvin,

I am not sure whether you, or anybody for that matter, takes handwritten submissions these days, but as I haven't got the means to do otherwise, I am submitting the enclosed "as is" for your consideration.

I don't know if you require background information from contributors, but for what it's worth, I am a schoolmaster and have had a number of poems and critical pieces published in magazines, scholarly journals, and in newspapers.

My good wishes,

John Oberon Greeve

IN VERMONT

It's not that it is old,
But that it's stopped.
Not appealing; arresting.
Yes, it engages:
It is easy to die here.

Aspects of it everywhere in magazines,
Used often to sell autumn,
One kind of Christmas card.
Easter does not come.

The storekeeper unrolling his awning
In no hurry in the morning light,
Saying "Mawnin', Elmer,"
Could very well be real.

A town drunk is possible.
He could loaf on a green.
A green is possible,
But still, shadowed.

Central and impervious, on higher ground,
An Inn offers its outsized porch;
Here, there, out of the cluster
A steeple enters autumn sky.

Against the afternoon chill
A town huddles itself together,
Grows heavy in its stone,
Still as a picture,
Half a notion.

Mr. Philip Upjohn
Director of Studies
Wells School
Wells, Connecticut

Phil—

Have Arnold sweep the cobwebs out of the office marked "Greeve."

He is returning. No fuss or hoop-la please. I will cry and stutter. (Just kidding about Arnold. I know he'd never do it.)

Should arrive the 5th, possibly before this card.

Best,

J.O.G.

6 February

REMARKS TO THE SCHOOL

I have been gone so long that it actually feels a little strange standing in the old spot addressing you—strange, but better the longer I stand here. My job of course is to welcome you back after Christmas holidays, but I've forfeited that by quite a margin. Instead let me thank you for the wonderful welcome back you have given me. As you know from your own vacations, the longer you stay away, the harder it is to come back. I think I made it just in time.

I want to say just once, and briefly, although I will go on feeling it for as long as I live, that this school's support of my wife and of me during her painful illness and after is the most valued gift I have ever been given. Mrs. Greeve was deeply and happily devoted to this school from the day we joined it. On behalf of both of us, thank you.

Now there is some business that ought to be attended to. Due no doubt to my absence from the sidelines, the wrestling and basketball teams seem to have fallen, temporarily, on bad times. I have it on good authority from coaches Trefts and Tomasek that there is nothing wrong with our personnel, that with discipline, and with a few breaks, and especially with improved school support, there is not an opponent on the schedule we cannot beat. I like the sound of that. Let's do it.

Another concern is the state of our buildings: dorms, classrooms, library, and commons. The concern is that they are a mess. Even though snacks and beverages are not allowed in the formal commons rooms, I see potato chips tracked into the carpets and pop stains on upholstered furniture. These spaces are not only what guests and parents and prospective applicants see when they come to Wells, they are, more importantly, our living rooms. We live in them. The Wells I have in my head is an architecturally fine, sturdy, and, here and there, an *elegant* place, but the Wells I have seen since my return is tired and uncared for and uninviting. It has always been easy to let things go to seed during these grim February and March weeks, but we must not let it. I invite you to look over your rooms and the school's common spaces and see if you don't agree that we look a little uncared for. This is our job, our responsibility; we don't have any special staff to pick up after us.

Not unrelated to this concern is a reminder that this coming weekend is Parents and Alumni Winter Weekend. There will be more than twice our usual number among us in classrooms, in the dining hall, wherever they choose to roam. Let's do our best for these two crucial constituents of the school. Let's give them our best courtesy and show them our best face. That has been our tradition, and I am sure we are up to it.

Well, I am now feeling quite used to standing at this podium, and I daresay the novelty has worn off for you, too.

Have a very good morning.

6 February

MEMO
To: Phil Upjohn
From: J.O.G.
<u>Confidential</u>

Phil—

It occurs to me that my "spruce up" and Alumni Weekend
remarks may have been ill-considered from your standpoint.
I know you have done all the actual work setting up this
weekend, and I should perhaps have checked with you
before sounding this morning's curmudgeonly note. For
God's sake, please don't take anything I said as *critical* of
your heroic stewardship!

And let me know what you want from me in the way of
speaking and general gladhanding this weekend.

J.O.G.

P.S. Could you please give me an update on the classroom
performance of Ms. Armbruster? The schools placement
services have come up with nothing, and Kurt Kohler has
declined to do an encore, so we may be stuck with her for
the duration. Will that be endurable? I'd appreciate whatever info you can supply me, as I've asked her to come
over for an evaluation this afternoon. I plan to break her
defenses with sherry. If she can at least admit she's
having a tough time, we might be a giant step towards
conveying mathematics to boys. Help!

J.

8 February

Mr. and Mrs. Frank Greeve
14 Bingham Drive
Tarrytown, New York

Dear Val and Frank,

Somehow I am back. The New England Inns almost
swallowed me up, but I slipped away at last, like Aeneas
from Dido, at night.

I don't think anyone here has caught onto it yet, but I'm at sea (not like Aeneas, who had a destination). Oddly enough, the house is fine. It feels comfortable, and the familiarity of everything and the quiet (the faculty is still observing an implicit quarantine) are lifesaving. I've moved back into the master suite, Meg's sickroom, and even that is fine. School's the problem.

I tried not to overreact when I got back, but I probably did anyway, to the depressing squalor I found everywhere around me. There isn't a clean surface of furniture on the campus. Even in our best "formal" rooms, there is hardly an upholstered piece that is not stained, greasy, or otherwise awful. A few routine calls on boys in their rooms have left me appalled, and my concerned visits to the quarters of their respective housemasters left me equally appalled. The old prod, "Do you do that kind of thing at *home*?" probably no longer applies. I am sure they do that sort of thing at home—and that their parents do, too, that no one is "hung-up" or "uptight" about it anymore, that women are "liberated" from it and men are "laid back" about it and that everybody is impervious to litter and grit and stick and mar and to haphazard, designless rooms. Everybody but Greeve. They will haul me into their court and say, "Is that all you've got to think about in this age of imminent global catastrophe and spiritual impoverishment?" "No," I will throw back defiantly. "Except when I see a mess." Shot at dawn.

The struggle for even token decencies in an adolescent world is always a little Sisyphean, but I don't remember feeling before that the rock had rolled irretrievably away from me down the hill. I have gone so far as to pick up and to rearrange a few of the rooms myself, but the improvement is imperceptible.

There are other problems. I went yesterday afternoon to do a guest stint on some Frost poems for a fifth-form English class and was sorely troubled by the state of the class. I arrived to find a startlingly aromatic seminar of a dozen boys and teacher, most of the boys reclining almost horizontally around the table. For comfort, some of them had slipped out of their shoes. Lest you think I am a terrifying presence in the school, I assure you that no adjustments in posture—in fact few signs of recognition—were made as the headmaster entered the classroom. The teacher, reputedly a good one and very popular, introduced me and the day's business for about five minutes in one continuous, hopeless sentence, each imperfectly related clause connected to the last by the phrase "in terms of." What has happened to speech? Without clear, logical speech, everything goes—writing, even thought. I started into Frost and got through little more than a read-through when up went the hands and out came the interpretations. I heard three or four different kinds of jargon, including a heavy dose of psychoanalytic stuff. The teacher, apparently delighted by such precocity, beamed encouragement. In one of the poems a "luminary tower" housing a clock appears. This I was told was clearly a phallus. What, I asked, is a big phallus doing towering over this particular town, and what does it add to the theme of the poem, which seems to be loneliness? The boy faltered, but his teacher came to the rescue saying that in terms of the whole phallic *principle,* a protrusive tower, aggressively thrusting itself out of the town's order could be seen as a rejection of that order in terms of the kinds of things the narrator was experiencing. On we went in this vein for about an hour, the teacher reinforcing the boys' muddled talk and thinking whenever possible. At one point, in desperation, I began recording their interpretations on the chalkboard, stanza by stanza, so that the lack of coherence and some of the hilarity of what they were saying would be more obvious. They were unfazed. They were perfectly willing to see Frost as a sower of great phalluses among a garden of unrelated literary devices. No one brought one of those *relatively straightforward poems* home to understanding. We made no contact with Frost. Afterwards with the teacher, I equivocated, speculated politely as to what I supposed the boys had tried to do with the poems, raised in an avuncular way the possibility of missing the *point* of a poem through too much sophistication. Etc. Sophistication! He told me that in terms of their critical understanding of literature, his goal was for them to "take risks." I could think of nothing to do in the face of this but to drink, which is what I did.

I cannot even claim to be physically tired anymore. I get *loads* of rest, so much so that it is getting hard to sleep. I am sure this is temporary, but for the moment, I must confess I haven't got the heart for school. All you have to do is to tilt the lens the smallest bit and everything is transformed into a new, sinister clarity. Kids are revealed as furtive, unkempt, unhelpful. Faculty settle for unattractive behavior and for third-rate performance. The school food looks, smells, *is* horrible. And there is no way of changing any of it without changing all of it. For that matter, what did anybody ever *expect* with adolescents? They have throughout human experience been the most irritable, least governable class of person. Why hole up hundreds of them together? Why boys? I cannot answer any of these fundamental questions regarding my work. My experience does not convince me that adolescent boys are better off leaving their households, neighborhoods, and communities, where tentative self-identifications, relationships, and responsibilities have begun to be forged, in order to go off to rather oddly structured hothouses where those crucial processes are interrupted, in some cases never to be continued. I'm not saying that boarding schools don't know what they're doing; I'm only saying that I don't know what I'm doing. And what is more, I don't know anything else either. I have learned over the past couple of days that I have no special moral strength; in short, nothing has accrued.

Gloom. Self-pity. Noise. Disregard all of it. I'm in a new treatment program called Writing Therapy. My own invention, actually. Does wonders, but bores the relatives.

It's late. Good night.

Love,

John

MEMO
To: Phil Upjohn
Director of Studies

9 February

Phil:

My verdict is that Florence is human. With some depart-
mental support and with our conspicuous presence now
and then in her classroom, she'll get through the year,
and mathematics will be taught.

Let's be nice to her.

J.O.G.

11 February

Mrs. Faye Dougan/PARENTS' VIGIL
1995 Wisconsin Avenue, N.W.
Washington, D.C.

Dear Mrs. Dougan,

I have only the sketchiest idea of what your organiza-
tion does, but I have been told that you have outreach
centers abroad through which you try to locate missing
and runaway children. If this is what you do, I would like
to apply for your services.

My son, Brian Greeve, aged 22, took off on an open-
ended trip abroad nearly a year and a half ago. He
seemed to tour western Europe from hostel to hostel, for a
month or so before gravitating to Spain, Portugal, and
then North Africa. He wrote periodically for several months,
asked twice for money. I last heard from him about a year
ago. The letter was postmarked Cape St. Vincent, Portugal,
which looks on the map to be a coastal village. I have
since written to him there several times and received no
response. A money order sent there has not been claimed.
I have contacted U.S. embassies in Morocco, Spain, and
Portugal, but they have found nothing.

Can you help? Have you got finding agents abroad? In

154

the countries I have named? If you can help me, I will be glad to pay whatever finding fees are involved. Brian has been no stranger to drugs and their devotees. Centers of that sort of activity may be fruitful places to start looking.

My son is unaware that his mother became ill and recently died. It is very important that I get in touch with him.

I enclose some photographs for identification purposes. Please do not hesitate to call me if I can provide you with further information that may assist you in finding him.

Yours sincerely,

John Greeve

14 February

MEMO
To: Phil Upjohn
Director of Studies

Dear Phil,

I am sorry our talk yesterday p.m. devolved into unpleasantness. I do not wish to salt wounds here, but there are some premises that ought to be cleared up so as to avoid occasions for such unpleasantness in the future.

First, let me repeat: you are *not* at fault for the concerns I raised about the parent/alumni weekend. I am clearly and principally at fault. The orchestrating of that show has always been my responsibility, and I neither took it on, nor shared with you the tried-and-true procedures necessary to insure that it went its best. Returning to the campus with term in full swing, I felt (wrongly!) reluctant to storm in and to tread on plans already made. This was a mistake. The tone of those kinds of affairs is primarily my responsibility, and I should not have stayed in the wings, treading be damned. You may disagree with me here, but there I stand. This is not the same thing as saying you are somehow unable to manage a parents' weekend. I don't think this for a minute. I do think, though, that some guidance was required on this last one.

Here are some guidelines for future weekend affairs, whoever is in charge.

1 • An agenda of all parent-related weekend events should be printed and provided to all visiting participants; these should be available at guest houses and hotels and should be everywhere available on this campus.

2 • All visitors' time should be provided for, theoretically. This means that even if parents don't visit classes or don't attend this or that faculty talk, there should be some plausible attraction: coffee and cake at Hallowell House, student-art exhibit at Gibbs, exercise clinic at the field house, etc.

3 • Faculty should be available in offices for parent chats. Times and locations should be printed and posted.

4 • Student guides, preferably clean ones, should be recruited from Gray Key and from other organizations.

5 • Overall, events should be bridged with some sort of attraction. If the Guests' Supper is over by seven and the musical doesn't begin till eight, wheel out the glee club, the octet, or some endearing home-made ensemble.

6 • A pre-weekend faculty meeting is always in order to run through the steps of the weekend program. Both faculty and students must be prepared. Everybody is more gracious when we sense a proper occasion is upon us and when we feel informed about what's going on.

We cannot be embarrassed about doing "PR"—we should only be embarrassed about doing it falsely or badly. Our parents and our alums are our lifeline. It is essential that they feel *positively impressed* with how we run things, especially their things. If someone drives a full morning up here from New York only to be confused, bored, cold, and seated uncomfortably at perhaps not too good a meal, those impressions go deep. These people are our clients. They have options. If not with their enrolled son, then maybe with the next one, or the nephew, or the neighbor. If we keep our fairly substantial light under a bushel for our parents and alums, we could easily dry up as a first-line school in five years.

I don't mean to lecture you, Phil, but I *care* about this issue, and I guess I want you to share that concern. Let's not have it be a me-you thing. At any rate, we'll dazzle them at commencement.

What was that play again? *Tiny Murders*? *Little Murders*? Not only the most ill-performed show I have ever seen here, a thoroughly vulgar thing too. What luck. Not characteristic Burgermeister.

J.

14 February

MEMO
Mr. Robert Burgermeister
Theatre Department

Bob—

Far from me ever to question a Burgermeister decision, but was *Little Murders* appropriate stuff for us? For our parents/alumni? Is that frothy comedy these days? Is there a laugh in the show? Is the bathroom stuff funny?

I feel comfortable raising these questions only against my previous record of unrestrained approval of all Burgermeister stage work. Take this for what it's worth.

J.O.G.

16 February

REMARKS TO THE SCHOOL

Gentlemen: Not much more than a week ago I stood before you to say a few things by way of getting reacquainted. One of the things I said was that I was glad to be back. Another was that I was concerned about the amount of casual destruction I saw on the campus.

I would like to update those remarks. This morning I am less glad to be back. Apparently a few of you took my statement of concern as a kind of challenge. Since then the following events have occurred: all of the corridor light bulbs on the first floor of Gibbs have been smashed, the pay phone in the commons has been ripped out—the only phone available to under formers for outside calls— and, this one you all have, I am certain, already had a good laugh about: the oldest and most valuable work of art in the school has been permanently damaged.

Let's look for a moment at the last one, the funny one. It must have been hilarious—and daring too—to bash a great hunk out of the genital area of the statue. Imagine it, the *private parts!* It worked, too. Whoever did it knew his—knew their—school. There has been a lot of laughter and excited comment since Sunday night. And if the deed was meant to say, "Take *that,* school and authority!", that worked too. At least it worked with me. I took it, and was alternately dumbfounded, furious, and helpless. It was certainly an effective and dramatic act.

As many of you know, it's right out of the history books, too. Somebody, whether Corinthian troublemakers or Alcibiades and his thuggy friends, hacked off the genitals of the 'herms' of Athens just on the brink of the second war with Sparta. That stunt was effective also—shocking, outrageous, and, to the hip and cynical, hilarious. Although you will have to go to the history books to learn how, it also brought down the city of Athens, down from perhaps the height of any city in the western world before or since. It brought down Athens, brought down Alcibiades, brought down his innocent teacher, Socrates, and it brought down the thugs and cynics who started it all.

You know, boys, it *means something* to strike out at your own symbols.

Statue of a Boy was given to Wells by Thomas R. Wade, member of the first graduating class of the school. The statue has been in the vestibule of Wells House for over seventy years.

Thomas Wade left Wells and made a career as a distinguished journalist before Woodrow Wilson appointed him ambassador to Italy, during which service he purchased the sculpture he would later give to us. *Statue of a Boy* is a fifteenth-century Roman reproduction in marble of a Hellenistic statue still in Rome. Valued, until Sunday night, at about a quarter of a million dollars, it represents a direct line of Western idealism from classical Greece through the Italian Renaissance to the twentieth century. The statue is—was—said to represent "the finest of human possibilities in the figure of a youth."

So much for human possibilities. The Wells campus, incidentally, is as I reported to you last week: a seedy, sticky mess. And as long as I'm so full of history this morning, I'd like to record a bit of present history. Today, February 16, 19—, Wells School is a third-line independent school for boys. Good morning.

16 February

MEMO
To: Tomasek, Upjohn, All Housemasters

Colleagues,

Let's meet in my office briefly as soon after seventh-hour class as possible. Agenda: to free boys from sports or other commitments for the time it takes to clean this place up!

J.O.G.

19 February

Mr. Raymond Taskich
Vice President, Operations Group Division
Jersey Standard, Inc.
440 Third Avenue
New York, New York

Dear Mr. Taskich,

Thanks so much for your visit and for sharing with us the corporate view of the energy situation. Enclosed is our modest honorarium; please let me know what expenses you incurred coming up here, and we shall reimburse you at once.

As we discussed, the question-and-answer session was tough, but I hope not unpleasant. I disagree that our boys and faculty are "overloaded" on the environmentalist side. If the questions on taxes and profits and oil-company influence on public policy seemed especially pointed, it was not because we were in some way gunning for you; I think rather that the polemical mood was invited by the very strong and unequivocal position you took about the inadequacy of alternative sources of fuel and energy use. Your point, if I have it correctly, is that without fossil fuel or its equivalent at roughly present levels of consumption, there would be a decline in both the gross commercial output and in the quality of American life.

I think the boys bought the first premise—that fuel is the basis of a good deal of the secondary activity of the economy—but they were less willing to accept the second premise: that diminished national consumption was equivalent to a diminished quality of life. I am neither an economist nor an ecologist, but it seems to me that there is a case to be made for less being not necessarily worse. If there is something wrong with this position, I think the boys would be receptive to arguments that pointed it out. Some of your respondents were at first puzzled and then a little angry when you classed them with the "sixties commune crowd" or with Mr. Solzhenitsyn. Most of your audience was newly born when the "sixties commune crowd" was a cultural factor; I'm not sure what, or if, they think about Solzhenitsyn.

I hope you would agree that the boys took you and your position seriously and that they cared about the questions they asked. Frankly, I found the exchanges, even at their most crackling, very thought-provoking, and the discussion here continues.

We thank you for that and for providing us so much stimulation.

My good wishes,
John Greeve

Mr. Dewey Porter
Chairman, Seven Schools Conference
The Adelbert School
Eavesham, Connecticut

Dear Dewey,

I received your letter this a.m. and then tried to reach you by phone—futilely, which perhaps is a good thing. Let me in writing try to sort out my thoughts about the recent Seven Schools business.

In effect, Wells has been given an ultimatum: either to schedule St. I.'s into next year's athletic program or to be excluded ourselves from the Seven Schools Conference. Let me tell you why from here this smells of a power play—and of a fundamentally unfair one at that.

1 • Why wasn't Wells invited to be a party to this "Seven Schools" decision?

I know I was away (sorry, I can't seem to stick to business this winter), but Phil Upjohn was here plenipotentiary, and our athletic director Dave Tomasek has always been invited to Seven Schools meetings. Why were we, certainly the most interested party, excluded?

2 • Your proposed decision effectively puts us out of the league and destroys our year's interscholastic program— since, as I wrote you this past fall, we have already rescheduled for next year; we could not reschedule St. I.'s even if we wanted to. And given what has transpired (the original issue), we do not want to. Nor would any other school that has an interscholastic sports policy.

3 • I am curious how in your mind the solution proposed fits the initial problem. If you recall, all that we asked from Fred Maitland was an *acknowledgement* that a dirty game had been a dirty game. We never claimed they were solely at fault or asked them to eat any crow. We asked them to *acknowledge* that a game in which boys squared off and belted each other, cursed each other and the officials, incurred penalties in malice—we asked them to *acknowledge* this as a poor show.

St. I.'s would not accede to our relatively manageable sanction of curtailing competition with them for a year, but you ask us to knuckle under to sanctions that would leave us without a sports program for the coming year. *4* • I'm confused about your repeated references to the "unilateral" actions of Wells as the cause of all subsequent problems. Didn't *I* bring the problem to Seven Schools attention by calling you about it on October 4, writing you about it on October 15, and several times since? What could have been more open than our concern about what happened, what we wanted to do about it, what we did about it?

I think that is enough. Is there a *principle* involved in this decision, Dewey? What is it?

Faithfully,

John Greeve

23 February

MEMO
To: Florence Armbruster
Mathematics

Florence—

By all means—as before?

J.O.G.

25 February

Mr. William Truax
President, The Fiduciary Trust Company
P.O. Box 121
New Haven, Connecticut

Dear Bill,

I am as impressed with the currency of your information about recent Wells developments as I am disturbed about the substance of your letter.

I am as surprised by the Seven Schools decision as you are. I am sorry you had to learn about it through scuttlebut instead of from me. My plan was to get Dewey Porter at Seven Schools to elaborate the situation further (my letter enclosed) and then pose some alternative responses to the board. As you will not fail to detect in my letter to Dewey, I think the decision stinks. It was concocted in the dark, and there's no principle in it.

All is not necessarily lost. We can:

1 • Tough it out. Rescheduling the seasons without our Seven Schools rivals will be a monumental task, given our relative isolation, and given the time of year, but if we make a project out of it, we can do it. Two things are in our favor here: (1) Dave Tomasek's stock is very high in the area and in the state, other A.D.s will do him favors, and (2) we have a principle; some schools will appreciate this, and we might even find ourselves with new friends and the subject of a feature story or two. This alternative involves the most risk and the most unknowns, but there is some element of goodness in it.

2 • Bide our time and urge Seven Schools to equivocate. They don't want to reschedule either, for the same reasons we don't. Only St. I.'s is really out of joint about this. If enough discomfort and inconvenience surface in the near future, I suspect Dewey could get St. I.'s to put together some sort of not-too-cringing acknowledgement of last fall's fiasco. I've phoned all but one of the other heads, and nobody is passionate about expelling us— seem even a little embarrassed about the whole thing. They should. This is the political solution. It is easiest, but the outcome is not certain, and it could cost us valuable time.

3 • Slink back on the terms suggested. This would involve cancelling those games and matches already made that might conflict with St. I.'s contests. This is very poor form and reflects badly on Tomasek and the school. Filling St. I.'s into the cracks of existing schedules causes other problems and expenses; we are only budgeted for what we already have. This solution's only merit is convenience. It affirms foul play at one level and power plays at another. There is nothing good in it. Our faculty could probably live with it. I couldn't and wouldn't. How about you?

Your second and third concerns trouble me even more. I am sorry that my December-January absence delayed the Stone-suit proceedings, but I think it's madness to make any kind of settlement with her out of court. Not only, as in the St. I.'s business, would a poor principle—*no* principle—be served, it would set a really destructive precedent for our disciplinary process, which happens to be an unusually fine one. Perhaps I should phone Seymour myself, but I cannot imagine Mrs. Stone really wants this litigation. I'm sure she would slink away if she were sure we were ready to go to court. If we do go to court, we will certainly win. As I understand it, and I have taken some pains to understand it, all we are obligated to do as a private institution is to carry out whatever disciplinary process we say we carry out. We certainly did this with Charles Stone and the other litigants. We don't do our fellow schools any favors by running away from this confrontation. So let's not. If, as you fear, the case generates publicity in the northeast, it will be publicity about a school *taking a stand* on the right side of an issue that bothers most parents. This would help rather than hurt us in the long run.

I am bothered most by the *basis* of your concern about the Stone business. I don't like your implication that things are going to smash here because of "a drug mess, a drowning, a serious athletic squabble, an increasingly doubtful admissions picture, and so on." "And so on"? Those incidents, although sad in themselves, are absolutely typical of what happens in schools, including great schools. A good school isn't good because there are no incidents; it is good because of the way it responds to them. Without distorting the facts, I could make any year at Wells look worse than this one. The flack you've been getting from "a number of alumni" is left over from a flat, half-assed alumni weekend we had earlier this month in the February Gloom. I wasn't quite back in the saddle then, and we botched it. See who among your complainants feels the same way after commencement.

Two points of substance before closing. (1) I haven't forgotten "Wells: Ten Years and After." Wish I could. (2) Back to the Stone business, please urge Seymour and others not to back off from the confrontation.

You asked me, with respect to school policy, if it would matter too much if I curtailed the practice of announcing and discussing major disciplinary results before the school. Seymour told me in the fall the precedent has recently gone against this practice as defamatory to students and their families. This is bad legal precedent and betokens only poor legal work on behalf of some schools' lawyers. The most positive consequence of any discipline decision in a school is processing it out through the school community. You share it. You make it part of the students' collective experience. In this way preposterous rumors are squelched, and some actual moral lessons are learned. You tell the students all about what happened and why, because you are not ashamed about what you have done and so that the event can be an occasion for learning. No good school can do otherwise. This tradition has served us well for decades. Should it buckle for the likes of Mrs. Stone? Don't ask me to practice bad medicine for bad reasons.

Faithfully,

John

P.S. Could you get me some sort of board consensus on the Seven Schools decision when it is convenient?

J.

Mr. and Mrs. Frank Greeve
14 Bingham Drive
Tarrytown, New York

Dear Val and Frank,

Thanks very much for your nice offer to have me come down there and relax for a weekend. For what sense it makes, I don't have enough energy to gear up for a weekend of relaxation. Nor, I'm afraid, the time.

If the truth be known, things are not quite going smoothly here. We're getting thrown out of our athletic league for good sportsmanship, we are being taken to court for practicing consistent discipline, and I have just received a long, passionate letter from a man from Jersey Standard who says I need to learn about the real world.

This is a depressing time of year, extra depressing due to school circumstances, extra depressing due to personal circumstances. Everywhere I look I see mess.

I have no business writing in this mood.
Another weekend?
Write and tell me about Hugh, Jill, summer plans?

Love,

John

28 February

MEMO
To: Tim Spires
Hallowell House

Tim:

All we need!

Why not give the boy one more chance, alone, with you, to say where he got the stuff and who else at Wells was involved. Although it all sounds relatively straightforward to me, please write down a thorough account of how you found him and his explanation for what he did, etc. When you are finished with him, bring him to me.

Extra effort much appreciated.

J.O.G.

28 February

MEMO
To: Phil Upjohn
Director of Studies

Phil—

Tim Spires walked in on a Hallowell Boy, David Weisman, smoking pot in his room. He's worked him over pretty thoroughly, and in an hour we'll know about all we're going to know about it. Would you please assemble the Student Court and the Faculty Discipline Committee. They ought to meet at their earliest convenience, tonight if possible. I will see to isolating the boy and calling his parents.

Wonderful timing, eh?

J.O.G.

28 February
Midnight

Mr. Jake Levin
R.D. 3
Petersfield, New Hampshire

Dear Jake,

Good to get your letter. Sorry to have been so long out of touch, but things have been a little crazy here since I got back.

It's a little strange, actually. The problems have been quite ordinary, which is not to say unimportant, school problems, but for some reason they won't be resolved.

167

Even when the right answer is obvious—at least obvious to me—it seems impossible to get a consensus, to act. That of course sounds vague, but I'd have to tell you too much more to make it any less so.

I have spent the earlier part of this evening interviewing a boy who was caught smoking pot in his room, after which I had the unsettling experience of talking to the boy's parents, both on the line at once, two of the most wretched-sounding people I have ever encountered.

I must be losing my heart for this work.

The first annoyance was my realization, when the boy was led into my study, that I didn't know him, that although we are a self-professed intimate community (our catalogue says so), I could not recall ever having laid eyes on this boy before. If I had, I would like to think I would not have allowed him to enroll. The overall impression was somehow unassignably canine. There was a lot of nose and chin and closely set dark eyes. He slouched when he stood, slumped when he sat, avoided looking at me. His attitude may have been surly or it may have been his natural way of expressing unease. Perhaps it was the pot. He was guileless in a way that made me wish he had guile. Yeah, he said, I was smokin'. Yeah, he said, I know the rules. Yeah, he said, I thought about getting caught. I smoke pot, he said. I like it. Only then did he look directly at me, a look that was not quite defiant, but was at least detectably sure of itself. When I asked him where he got his pot, he told me: I found it around somewhere. Where? Around somewhere—outside. When I asked if he smoked with anybody else, he said no, never. He lied in the same flat, thick manner in which he told the truth. He was impervious to intimidation, also to instruction, also to inspiration. And the worst of it is that I didn't feel the slightest bit moved to try to intimidate, instruct, or inspire him. Although that is my professional duty. I sent him to the outer office and went through his file. He is a fourth former, entered as a third former. He had C's in his local middle school, where his guidance counselor noted that he was a good citizen who responded well to encouragement. Our admissions officer wrote: "seemed uncomfortable in interview, parents very aggressive, stressed how many other good schools were on their itinerary." Testing: top of bottom third independent school norms; derived I.Q. 118. Grades at Wells: 60-70 in all subjects except Spanish, which he fails each term. Activities: went out for third-form football, was a back-up lineman, a reluctant practicer, quit mid-season claiming injuries. Discipline: quartered for smoking cigarettes last winter; minor discipline for failing to complete dining-hall assignments, Student Court for mauling, with others, a new third former this past fall. Expended to date at Wells: $14,000. Attainments: none.

I called the boy back in and made him sit down and sit up, directly in front of me. I looked dead into his pot-bleary eyes and said: I don't think this is going to sink in, but I'm going to tell you anyway. The reason we have strict rules against pot and other drugs is that they have taken boys we know on a one-way path to poor effort, poor performance, and bad, deep personal problems. This is not something we saw in a magazine. This is what happened to boys we know—to our school. It even happened to a boy in my family. You have not done anything special at Wells. You have been a weak student, and there are signs that you are getting weaker. You participate in very little, and you avoid assigned work. You cut corners. You disregard rules without much thought. You are doing a bad job. You are not growing up, except physically, and you are smoking pot. You smoke pot, and you like smoking pot. You like to smoke pot, and you are doing a bad job. Stop doing it. Stop doing it now.

I wished I were his father so I could have slapped him across his doggy face and shaken him till he cried. He waited me out.

They are all waiting me out, Jake.

Good night,

John

Mr. Dwight Nimroth
Editor, *Poetry Magazine*
1665 Dearborn Parkway
Chicago, Illinois

Dear Mr. Nimroth,

   I have enclosed a poem, "Lesson," for your consideration.
   I don't know if you require background information
from contributors, but for whatever interest it provides: I
am a schoolmaster and have published several poems and
some criticism in magazines, newspapers and literary
journals.

> My good wishes,
>
> John Oberon Greeve

LESSON

I have held you after class.
I have brought you to this dark place
Of my books and bachelorhood not to bore you
But to tell the truth:

Your work shows ordinary promise;
That is, no special promise;
That is, no promise.
Pressed for information, you volunteer
Fragments of what you have heard us say,
Of what you have, uncomprehending, read.

You stand as noise to an idea,
Inequipped to know the knock of right.
Subtlety, sides of a question surprise you,
Two answers confuse you.
The trickles of your talk
Flow from or into no known stream.

Beginning, even as a bright-faced child,
You lacked background.
Unable to assert, you guess.
Yet you are friendly,
You get by.

You may well be loved.
Others, pleased by your shape or smell
Will touch you and be touched.
Loosed from all certainty, often afraid,
You will assemble and speak out,
Find all of it familiar,
And sleep.

---

                                                    1 March

Mr. and Mrs. Nathan Weisman
12 Club Crescent
Garden City, Long Island

Dear Mr. and Mrs. Weisman,

I am writing to put formally the unhappy message I
had to bear over the phone earlier today: that our Student
Court and Faculty Discipline Committee have recommended
that David be dismissed from Wells for smoking marijuana on campus. As headmaster, I must accept the recommendation. The arrangements you suggested for picking him
up are fine; he is welcome to stay in my house till then.

I understand that it is properly parental to be upset by
an unexpected blow like this, but I am concerned about
some of the points you raised and would like to explain a
few matters of school policy. You, Mr. Weisman, advised
me that we had better "do with David as we have done
with the others." I assure you that we have done so, in
that we enforced a rule, the violation of which is a
published cause for expulsion, a rule David signed a
pledge to observe. What all boys get who break such rules

is a process, designed and periodically reviewed by the whole school. According to the process, offenders are assured of a hearing before an elected body of their peers and a faculty committee. That process, carried out as thoughtfully as we can, is what we guarantee to disciplinary offenders. During the past twenty years while we, like all schools, were trying to make sense of drug use among the young, the severity of penalties may have varied with prevailing thinking. Over the past five years, however, prevailing thinking, at least ours, has been firm: marijuana and school life are antithetical. With very few exceptions over that period, offenders, even first-time offenders, have been dismissed from school.

Your question, "Do we mainly catch Jews?" I choose to take straight. Memory tells me not, that a great majority of boys dismissed for drugs and other offenses are not Jewish. Memory will have to serve, as that is not an account we keep.

My deepest concern is that in your hurt and anger over all of this you have not responded to the possibility that David may have a problem with drugs. I honestly suspect this is the case. David came to us last year a boy with modest but acceptable potential; in short, with promise. We have seen very little development in him since then. In fact, he has appeared to us increasingly deadened, participating little, often verging on trouble. These things are as much danger signs as the joint in his hand when Mr. Spires caught him.

Believe me, these are not headmasterly pieties. We *lose* boys to marijuana. I have lost a son to marijuana. If David's departure from Wells and our combined concern about him are dramatic enough, we may provide an occasion for him to reverse a dangerous course in his development.

I sincerely hope this is the case.

Faithfully,

John Greeve

REMARKS TO THE SCHOOL

This past fall it was my unpleasant duty to talk to you about some boys who had gotten themselves in trouble with drugs. There were five of them, and as things turned out, all five were dismissed from Wells. We take time to talk about such things in chapel and we make hard decisions about such things for two basic reasons. First, we want to create an environment in which learning and personal development are most likely. The second is that we want to discourage others from following the path of those in trouble.

Apparently the October incident and the October talk were not adequate deterrents. We have lost another boy from Wells, our sixth this year. The boy is a fourth former, David Weisman. He was caught smoking marijuana in his room by a faculty member who smelled it two corridors away in his own study. The disciplinary proceedings were fairly uncomplicated, as there was not much in dispute. Mr. and Mrs. Weisman are of course upset and are on their way here to pick up David and his things.

As I said, the disciplinary procedures went without a hitch. However, some troublesome issues linger on. David admits that he likes to smoke pot. I suppose he has smoked on and off since he arrived. His pot comes from somewhere, very possibly from other boys here. He has probably smoked pot with other boys here. To do so he certainly had to be deceptive. He certainly must have lied. I'm not sure how many of you know David Weisman, but we are a small school, and certainly a good many of you do. Those of you who know him—perhaps a hundred or so of you—know that he hasn't gone in for much in the way of activities here, perhaps wasn't invited. You know that he hasn't done well in his studies. You know that he has been in periodic disciplinary scrapes, usually for avoiding things. And you know that he smokes marijuana. You know these things and perhaps find it hard to care about them.

I am starting to think I don't know very much about the drug problem in our school; and as to the caring problem, I haven't a clue as to what to do about that one. Maybe together we can work on those things. Otherwise there will soon be another David Weisman missing from the ranks, and when that stops mattering, Wells ought to shut down and sell its assets.

Good Morning.

3 March

Ms. Lucille Emerick
N.A.S.S. Records Service
Box 1000
Princeton, New Jersey

Dear Ms. Emerick,

I have received your questionnaire materials, labeled ADMIN, but I am sorry to have to decline participation. Questionnaires tempt me to lie and to exaggerate, so I always avoid them. Yours, incidentally, is the longest I have ever seen.

Good luck to you. Happily, I am not representative of SCHOOL OR COLLEGE ADMINISTRATOR.

Sincerely,

John Greeve

4 March

MEMO
To: Dave Tomasek
<u>Personal</u>

Dave—

I don't think I've ever received a formal written document from you before!

I appreciate the thought and the quality of the deliberations you and the head coaches have gone through on this St. I/Seven Schools mess. Your recommendation certainly makes the most sense from the practical standpoint, but, unless I am missing something, it seems to back straight down from the original issue, which is the important one.

I don't want to be prideful or stubborn about this. Between us, I phoned Fred Maitland last week and said in effect: why not come off this silliness? How about even a note to Seven Schools acknowledging a rough game in September and pledging support for better things in the future? No cigar. So I find myself in the position of not wanting *his* pride and stubbornness, just because they are firm, to carry the day. See what I mean?

I know you and your staff did not arrive at your position lightly, Dave, and you certainly could not have presented it more graciously, either in the conference, or in what you have written. But I am afraid I can't see it. Its justifying principle seems to be "the game must go on," which is good but not quite good enough.

This is not to say that you aren't right or even that you won't prevail, but it is to say that your solution is not one I can stand by in good faith as headmaster.

John

5 March

MEMO
To: All faculty and staff
Re: Pre-vacation cautions

Colleagues:

The alluring prospect of Spring Recess is upon us, and if tradition holds, the greatest incidence of disorder, bad feelings, snags, snarls, and tears will fall about now, unless we hedge against fortune in the next ten days.

As usual, Marge, Phil Upjohn, housemasters, and I have

175

put up heroic resistance to the barrage of parental requests to remove their boys, for compelling family and financial reasons, from Wells to the world's more vernal parts. Because we always say no, it is essential that we run full steam here until the 15th. Classes must meet and meet productively until noon on Friday and dorm staff must be on hand for an hour or so after that to pack off their tenants. I will assume this to be the case unless I hear otherwise from you individually.

Some reminders:

1 • Collect all late work and papers and sit boys down for make-up exams and quizzes before the Recess. Letting these slide until afterwards is a source of unending trouble.

2 • Observe schedule of testing dates, so that boys aren't all doing tests and handing in papers at the same time. If there is a log-jam we haven't detected, see Phil Upjohn.

3 • Collect all outstanding fees, fines, and library books. Peg Detweiller tells me that the library stacks have never been more depleted due to overdue books and to books never checked out. I have trouble seeing why the latter is not simple theft. Would you please, both as teachers and advisors, urge boys to comb their rooms for books and to return them? It would be nice, at least for me, to avoid fire and brimstone on this one.

This has been a tough, grim stretch, and I am not speaking only for myself. If we can just see ourselves responsibly through the next ten days, the following seventeen (!) will be all the sweeter.

Thanks in advance,

J.O.G.

Mr. Edward Janeway
Who's Who in High School
17795 Front Street
Bloomington, Indiana

Dear Mr. Janeway,

I am sorry to be so late in responding to your inquiry, but there has been more than the usual crush of work here.

I am afraid I can supply no names or other information for your proposed directory. I do not see how you can tell "distinguished secondary school achievement" in a boy until he is at least fifty.

Good luck, though, with your project.

Sincerely,

John Greeve

7 March

Mrs. Sandra Searle
309 Rumson Road
Rumson, New Jersey

Dear Mrs. Searle,

I am sorry to be so late in responding to your kind letter, but there has been more than the usual crush of work here.

You do not mention what paper you read, so I have no idea of how my "stand" is represented. Whatever stand there is, however, is a school stand, and I am not sure that Wells differs much from other schools with respect to rules about student drug use. Nearly all schools forbid drug use. Where Wells may differ—and again I am not sure of the extent—is in the consistency of its response to violations. Although we like to keep options open for exceptional circumstances, we have generally dismissed boys who have violated the school's drug policy. That policy is made very well known to our boys and their families.

You praise our sternness in the face of so much permissiveness. I don't know about that. We come down hard on violators for the sole purpose of saving as many boys as we can from drugs' interfering with their maturity. Hard consequences deter. When we lose a boy, we don't feel terribly stern, but rather, having failed, a little sad.

It's still an uphill battle with drugs, isn't it?

You were kind to write.

My good wishes,

John Greeve

7 March

Dr. Louis Giannini
National Institute of Drug Abuse
Rockville, Maryland

Dear Dr. Giannini,

I am sorry to be so late in responding to your invitation for me to speak at your symposium, but there has been more than the usual crush of work here.

I must decline your kind invitation. The reasons are largely practical, but I am also convinced I have nothing extraordinary to say about "Designing a Drug Policy for Schools." To me the problem has always been easy to understand: Drugs impair the way students learn and the process of growing up generally. The solution has also been clear: to forbid drug use and to deal strongly with violators. I don't think there is a speech in that.

I would like very much to be able to hear first-hand the current professional thinking about youthful drug use, and I would like to send some faculty to the symposium.

I am honored that you thought of me in connection with

the June program, but, again, I have only the stodgiest sort of things to say.

My good wishes,

John Greeve

8 March

Mrs. Faye Dougan
President, PARENTS' VIGIL
1995 Wisconsin Avenue, N.W.
Washington, D.C.

Dear Mrs. Dougan,

Your letter was upsetting, but I thank you very much for sending it. In a few weeks you have been able to come up with more than my brother and I did working fairly diligently for over a year.

I have contacted the parties you indicated in Washington, and I have written the consulate in Tangier for the wallet. I understand the passport should remain there in case he shows up to claim it. I cannot understand how a lost passport and wallet could be kept by the police for the better part of a year without somebody trying to get in touch with American authorities, family, etc.

It is hard to feel encouraged by your find. If Brian is alive, I suppose he must, without passport and wallet, be in the vicinity of Tangier. Yet, as you point out, he could not work, bank, even check into a hotel without a passport and identification. If he is alive he must be living the most marginal sort of existence, begging even, if that is allowed. I should know more about that possibility before long.

I must also, as you cautioned, be prepared for the possibility that he is dead. If that has happened, why would there be no body? If he was killed by someone and disposed of, why would wallet and passport turn up? I am afraid I find all of the possibilities depressing. As is your disclosure that quite a few American and European kids pass into North Africa and are not heard from again.

I will, as you counsel, prepare for the worst. I thought I was prepared for the worst, but it keeps worsening.

Again, thank you.

Faithfully,

John Greeve

9 March

Mr. and Mrs. Frank Greeve
14 Bingham Drive
Tarrytown, New York

Dear Val and Frank,

More grim news. I received a letter from the Parents' Vigil people in Washington. They have had confirmed that about a *year* ago Brian's wallet and passport were turned in to the Tangier police. Thanks to Parents' Vigil, both are now in the American consulate there. The implications of this are mostly bad. The best is that, if he is alive, he should be findable, in or around Tangier. How he could be alive, how he could manage for so long without identification or passport is hard to imagine. A few American and British contacts who have been given photos have agreed to comb the seamier quarters of the city for Brian, and if they don't come up with something in a week or so, I've got the names of some people I can pay to look properly. Whatever they do or don't come up with, short of Brian, I'll go myself when school breaks in June. I should probably go next week. I'm afraid he's gone.

Spring Recess begins Friday, and I have decided to give Little House another try. I have a feeling it will turn off the noise I have been living with lately, or at least will replace it with other noise. At any rate, I'm going there. There will be a phone, maybe, by the 25th or so. I'm going to ask Jenkins to turn on the water and the gas, but he will probably refuse. If so, I'll live on raw shellfish, bathe and poop in the sea.

With that vivid picture, I shall leave you.

Best to Hugh.

Love,

John

12 March

Mr. William Truax
President, The Fiduciary Trust
P.O. Box 121
New Haven, Connecticut

Dear Bill,

Well!

Out to pasture, is it? Why do you say until September? Do you think I'll improve over the interim? Why do you say "rest and refreshment"? If you look closely at the period during which you find me "not myself," you will see that it follows on the heels of the longest period of "rest and refreshment" I have ever had during a school year. I came back to Wells in February, Bill, because rest and refreshment was about to open its roaring jaws and swallow me up. I *am* myself. The petulant child, the erratic performer up north is I, Greeve. What you are finding fault with is not Greeve redux, but Greeve full throttle, prime Greeve, Greeve as he is.

I hope you know that I am more than able to throw up justifiable defenses to all your claims. For one thing, I never pledged, nor would I ever pledge, to refrain from discussing disciplinary actions before the school. Moreover, you never insisted that I do so, you just asked. I'll have to hand it to you, though, Truax, you do have your antennae up. The reason I will not throw up my (formidable) defenses is that I frankly did defy you.

I wrestled quite consciously with the issue of discussing the Weisman boy before the school; it would have been

181

relatively easy not to. At one point I almost phoned you to get an opinion. Then I decided I wouldn't. I knew what you'd say (and see, you've said it), and I knew what I would do. I just went ahead—same sort of jaw I've been giving for twenty years. I fully expected the stink. Just wanted you to know.

The Seven Schools business is both crucial to the coming year and not important at all. At its nub it's just like the drugs/legal business. We're either going to stand by what we've always said is important about Wells, or we're going to be convenient. Convenience is easy and safe in these two instances, and evidently this appeals to you and to whomever you are talking to here.

You are right that there is something wrong with the tone of the place. This may be my fault. I'm not sure.

You are also right that I am behind in my board work. Contracts are late, budget is late, "Wells: Ten Years and After" is only embryonic. This is poor form. No excuses.

So out to pasture I go. Who knows about this? Everybody? Let's by all means get together first week in April, in New Haven. The finance committee should meet there, too, while we're at it.

By the way, please do *not* get an outside man to prevail over my Rest and Refreshment—unless you really want a new head. It would take him till September to find the xerox paper. Let Phil Upjohn do it. He's not terribly good "up front," as you business fellows like to say, but he's very savvy about Wells, and the faculty trust him. He can do everything, even the diplomatic stuff, if he's told what's expected.

So it's bugger off, Greeve, is it? I feel like Willy Loman: really liked, really well liked.

Faithfully,

John

MEMO
To: All Faculty

Colleagues:

Before we all depart for warmer climes, I want to thank
you for your extra effort in bringing this term to a tidy
conclusion. As I keep saying, it has not been an easy
term. I will not now catalogue my woes, except to acknowledge that there were woes. You, too, have had woes. I hope
each of you enjoys the break, enjoyment richly deserved.
Contracts will be awaiting you on your return. Sorry for
the delay. As I said, woes.

Adios,

J.O.G.

15 March

REMARKS TO THE SCHOOL

It strikes me that the next time you all assemble here
many of you will be burnt brown, and all of you will be
refreshed. It is easy to forget how important refreshment
is: the break in the routine, the sudden change in plans,
the surprise. I hope you find it a little refreshing that I
am not bawling you out for something this morning.
Various people have pointed out to me recently that I
seem to be stuck in that groove. My apologies.

This morning I am not going to warn or denounce or
complain. Rather, I would like to reflect for a moment on
what is an important coming together in the year's religious calendar: Easter and Passover. It is a shame this
year that the school's vacation rhythm scatters us all for
these sacred holidays. The two events may have more to
tell us than all of our other holidays combined.

Friday, April second, will be both Good Friday and
Passover, key moments in Easter and Passover weeks,
respectively. The two events falling on that Friday are not

a coincidence; they are, at their heart, the same event. As Western Studies students will so vividly recall, in mid-thirteenth century B.C., a reluctant upper-class Hebrew named Moses began a series of demonstrations to convince the Egyptian pharaoh to free the enslaved Hebrews from bondage and to allow them to seek their ancestral homelands. Pharaoh refused, and in response Moses was able either to visit a series of disasters upon Egypt or, as some historians think, to convince Pharaoh that a series of natural disasters was brought about by the Hebrews' god. At any rate, boils, locusts, frogs, foul water, and other harassments befell Egypt until finally a curse was placed upon first-born sons. Whether through disease or by the hand of the Angel of Death, Egyptian youths perished. Hebrew sons were saved, they believed, because they had dabbed the lintels of their doorways with the blood of sacrificial lambs. The Angel of Death therefore passed over their households. In a fit of depression, pharaoh, grieving the loss of his own son, let the Jews go.

You know the rest of the story. The Jews fled in a hurry, narrowly escaping, doubting bitterly that they would survive another generation. Yet through their struggle, they would develop what has been the most enduring religious code in the Western world.

A dozen centuries later another committed Jew, Jesus of Nazareth, would come to Jerusalem, as he and his family had done every year of his life, to celebrate Passover. Like Moses, he came to liberate his fellow Jews from bondage, but not bondage to the state; from, rather, bondage to selfish, shallow living. Like Moses, Jesus had a dramatic effect on people *at first,* but was doubted and betrayed by them later. Like Moses, Jesus would not live to see the fruits of his labors. In fact, Jesus had so offended the Hebrew establishment during his last Passover week, that, sensing trouble, he was forced to celebrate his Passover meal—his last supper—a day early and in secret.

This was Thursday. He seemed to know that the next day he would be lost to his friends and followers. The

Angel of Death would *not* pass over him, he told them, but he would be the sacrificial lamb whose blood would allow them to live. No one understood any of this, and Jesus was arrested, tried hastily, and killed in the most brutal manner the state could devise.

At this, Jesus's followers scattered or went underground. Three days later, in many different reports, they claim to have seen him again, resurrected and alive. Convinced of this miracle, they spread the word that their leader and teacher had conquered death. This was the message that began the early church.

In a way, the Exodus of Moses and the Resurrection of Jesus are both great triumphs—without them there would be no Judaism or Christianity. Yet they are odd triumphs. Both events required great suffering and the loss of their respective heroes. That suffering and loss are essential to life is still a great mystery; for both Jews and Christians it is the mystery at the very center of life.

At one point during Passover week Jesus tries to explain the mystery to his disciples. These are his words:

> *Verily, verily, I say unto you. Except*
> *a corn of wheat fall into the ground and*
> *die, it abideth alone; but if it die, it*
> *brings forth much fruit. He that loves his*
> *life shall lose it; and he that hate his life*
> *in this world shall keep it unto eternal life.*

This is what Jews and Christians celebrate in Passover and Easter. Have a joyful holiday.

Good morning.

17 March
Little House

Mr. Jake Levin
R.D. 3
Petersfield, New Hampshire

Dear Jake,

I am writing in trying circumstances, like Chatterton. I am huddled in the parlor of Little House before a blazing fire that is miraculously radiating no heat at all. I have been told knowingly that insulation makes a difference and that summer houses are strictly summer houses, but I had, until this evening, an elemental faith in fire. I'm going to sit here like this for about ten more minutes and then I'm going to get into the fire.

Strangest thing has happened, Jake. I've been relieved of command. Not quite sacked, because I'm supposed to be able to come back in September, but asked with consummate graciousness to get out of the way while some messes I made get cleaned up. In my defense I would say that a few of the messes are the kind you can be proud of. But that sort of thing doesn't carry much weight with the school's trustees. They are practical men of affairs and see in messes only mess. Out, gently, goes Chips. Everybody's very nice, really. The truth of the matter is that a few of the messes are going to rouse a fight and nobody wants to fight *me* because I'm bereft, etc.

I think people hope that I'll pull myself together. That's the problem, the point I can't get anybody to see. Except that I am bereft and rather a bag of bones to look at, I *am* pulled together. This is it. I won't think or behave better under other circumstances. Without Meg, I am less, but I always was, and there is never going to be more, not in September, not in purgatory. That is the unsettling thing, not the enforced rustication. There were days I would have treasured a paid leave from March till Labor Day.

In those days I would have said, Ah, an opportunity To Write. Even would have Written—the stuff you always

186

found embarrassing and strident. I remember the time I was really mad at you for your non-interest in some things I had shown you and angrily gave you my artistic manifesto—that poems are to *celebrate* experience. To which you said, only if the experiences are worth celebrating. Damn. I used to think, and Meg agreed, that I was right and you were wrong, that I liked the world better than you did, that I was more open to inspiration than you were. I thought you were intentionally closing off to Goodness, Warmth, and supermarket epiphanies out of some left-over Beat affiliation. I thought you were trendy. I still think you are trendy, Jake, but you are also very healthy, and you are alive. I also thought, and told Meg to mark my words, that you would stop writing poetry altogether; without the Goodness, Warmth, etc., you'd dry up. Whereas Matthew Arnold and I, hand in hand, would prevail.

"We still had Thyrsis then—"

I don't mind that I was naive and wanted to *celebrate*— that's a rare and very useful state of mind for a school. I don't even mind that I was clumsy and mannered in the attempt. But I do mind that the experiences, both the concrete and the mysterious ones, I was so eager to celebrate might only have been projections of my own, smug, Meg-fortified self. The test of that would be to see if, when all bases for smugness were dried up, when all the props were knocked away, I could still celebrate. If I could do that, even a little, then something objectively true, some non-Greeve force would be pulling the celebration through my meager powers of invention. Then my poems would be objectively true, as I've always wanted to believe. Well, I fail the test. All the props have fallen away, and I'm dead as a dead fish, as T.S. Eliot once said about Edith Wharton. I can't celebrate anything. I can't even eat a whole sandwich. When I stick up for the old things at school—easy things, obvious things—I am not

convincing, I make people tired. This will not improve by
September.

This is what it means to die, I think. Only I have the
dubious privilege of being pellucid about it instead of
slipping into it senescently. I am all I am ever going to be,
and it's not enough, even for me.

Do you realize you never came down to Wells for a
reading? Why did we both let that go?

My love to you, old friend,

John

19 March

Mr. Dwight Nimroth
Editor, *Poetry*
1665 Dearborn Parkway
Chicago, Illinois

Dear Mr. Nimroth,

Not too close, I hope, on the heels of the other one, I am
enclosing a poem for your consideration.

My good wishes,

John Greeve

UNTHINKABLE AS

What is left, hours later, on the plate.
There is a way.
There are as many ways
As junk mail,
As hair color, as hair color goes,
As vision goes
Black
Or flesh sags under bone,
Bones sag under clothes;
As bones.

Hear, O shoppers
The manic little melody
Of a manic little angel
Flying just behind the ear;
She shadows, she shadows
Each memory and dream.
Grim jingle in the brain.
It could go on for days
This way,
There are so many ways.

John Oberon Greeve

---

26 March
Little House

Mrs. Florence Armbruster
22 Pie Alley
Torrington, Connecticut

Dear Florence,

I am so sorry for the mess. You were very sweet to come see me but you should not have come. I am not fit for visitors, certainly not for you. You are still warm. I am fortune's fool. Do you know that line?

You will see what I mean.

Bless you,

John

Mr. Clifford Bennett
Trust Department
The Fiduciary Trust Company
New Haven, Connecticut

Dear Cliff,

Thanks for all the time on the phone. I've drawn up a fair semblance of what you said would go down in the courts. It's basically very simple; the important thing, I think, is that you and others at the Fiduciary are clear of the intent. Here is the gist.

Upon my death I would like my wife's and my share of Little House and the yawl, the *Valmar,* which we also owned conjointly with my brother Frank, to go to him and his wife. The rest, such as it is, should be divided as follows: one-third to Wells School for whatever purposes they may choose; the other two-thirds I would like you to hold in trust for seven years for my son, Brian, who has been a missing person for some time, but possibly not lost; if after seven years Brian has not claimed his share, then I would like to give it to my nephew Hugh Greeve, my brother Frank's son.

Enclosed is a more formal statement of this arrangement witnessed as you stipulated by Herb Jenkins, proprietor of East Sandwich Boatyard. Herb has also notarized it.

I have also written and sealed a letter to my son which I would like my executors to hold for him until what time, if any, he can be found.

I thank you once again, Cliff, for the impeccable service you have given my family, especially since Meg's passing. You d_____ work credit.

Sincerely,

John Greeve

DISPOSITION OF ESTATE

I, John Greeve, being of sound mind and sure judgment, do hereby make on the date indicated below, the following disposition upon my death of my effects and possessions and of all property, revenue, dividends, and interest owned by me or due me.

1 • My share of the property of Little House, number 9 Ticonsett Lane, East Sandwich, Commonwealth of Massachusetts, shall pass to my brother, Francis Greeve of Tarrytown, New York.

2 • My share of the yawl, *Valmar*, shall likewise pass to my brother, Francis Greeve.

3 • A partition of one-third of my remaining estate shall, in a manner determined and directed by executors appointed by the Fiduciary Trust Company of New Haven, be given over to Wells School, Wells, Connecticut, as a gift. I understand that no special purpose or qualification shall impede the use of this gift by Wells School. Wells School may receive this gift in furniture, library documents, vehicles, or other portable property; or as cash value from such property sold at auction; or as cash and securities from my estate. The determination of the partition, the management of auction or auctions, and the transfer of all cash and securities will be directed by my executors.

4 • The remaining share of my estate, in no way including or overlapping the dispositions stated in items one, two, and three, shall pass to my son, Brian Greeve, provided he is located and can make a claim to this disposition within seven years from the date of this document.

If after seven years no claim is made by my son on this part of my estate, it shall pass forthwith to my nephew, Hugh Greeve.

This statement was composed in the presence of Herbert Jenkins of East Sandwich, Massachusetts on March 31, 19—.

(Signed)
John Oberon Greeve
March 31, 19—

(Witnessed)
Herbert Paul Jenkins
March 31, 19—

(Notarized)
Herbert Paul Jenkins
March 31, 19—

31 March
Little House

Dear Brian,

In earlier letters to you, unclaimed and unanswered, I tried to explain how hard it was expressing things to someone who might not be there. In the event you are there and one day read this, you will know what I mean.

If/when you come home, you will want information, history. Frank and Val will have that. Rely on them for as long as you need. Both of them care about you. I do want you to know, though, that tonight I am fairly clearheaded, although not too hot physically. I am steady about your mother's loss this past winter, steady but not "adjusted" to it.

The most recent intelligence I have on you is that your wallet and passport were turned in to the police a year ago in Tangier. A lady in an agency told me to expect the worst, which I do.

I am not a desperate man, the way you might think of one in a movie or in a Poe story. I feel used up, overcome, gnawn on, by irritations which, if I admit them fully to consciousness, will turn out to be the Furies themselves. What I am trying to say, Brian, is that I am not crazy. But I am finished.

This is even harder than I thought. Now my head is full of you, memories of you. Memories of all of us. A pitiful image of you keeps cropping up, like something in Dickens: you return this summer with your knapsack, sunburnt, cheery, perhaps even with a pal or a girl, to surprise Meg and me, maybe even to make some sort of end-of-adolescence, commencement-of-manhood reconciliation, only to find that your mother and I have, as the Wells boys say, checked out. Just a picture, not what I think will happen, not even, necessarily, what I want. It's a picture to hurt myself with, because I can't imagine, should that scene ever happen, your being able to handle it. It is a picture of you as me now. Me not you. Every bubble bursts back to me. It should make me sad not to believe in the picture—the part about your coming home gladly to see us—but I don't. I don't think you are alive, Brian. I don't think that you are glad or were ever glad in your travels. I think you are dead and that you died in terror, possibly not in your right mind. I don't think you thought much about your mother and me, which is not to say that we weren't crucial anyway. I think your runaways, your school rebellions, your silences, your frightening flights of fantasy when you were little—I think all of them were ways of negating us. Now we are negated, but by our own demons and diseases, not by you. You hurt us, Brian, because you wouldn't let us know how we hurt you. You hurt us, but you didn't kill us. May you live.

Your mother was 34 and I was 33 when we had you. There had been lots of gynecological problems and failures, but then it finally worked. No child was ever more wanted. But we were aware of that, and like intelligent educators steeped in child-development, we vowed not to smother you. From the beginning you were given real liberty—and we watched in fear for liberty to fail. Did it? Or was it the watching and the assessing and the knowing on our parts? Maybe granting liberty negates the liberty. I'm back to "negates." I wish I knew the answers. I was only the father of you, just that once. I was not really very confident about it. I think I was a good teacher, a very good teacher (why be modest?). As a teacher and usually as a headmaster, I was very sure, which made me seem even strong at times. But not as a father. As a father, I always felt I was guessing. I felt I was guessing and felt you knew I was guessing. I didn't know whether to hit you or hold you, whether to make you turn out the light and go to sleep or to turn up the light so you could see what you were doing. What *did* I do? I think I generally went on down the hall, thinking about it. Thinking a lot about it. Oh, Brian! What I wanted was for you to be admirable without ever being told to or told how—to surprise me with your brains and skill and splendid qualities, qualities that would burst forth simply because you were ours and we were good. I wanted you to be happy, one-of-a-kind, passionate, imaginative. I wanted to follow your happiness and be happy about it, like the dads whose hearts thrill in the stands when their sons hit a long ball. Any old kind of long ball would have been fine with me. But you sensed me in the stands. I was not only a dad in the stands but a headmaster in the stands. I don't like to think about that.

I was glad to be head of Wells, Brian. I think I was good at it, and I think people who know thought I was good at it. I was better than old-fashioned. Like Socrates, but less purely, I had my "little voice" and it told the hard truth. I also had something else that was good for a school—I loved the culture. Not everything, not the whole mess, but the triumphs of its building, its pictures, its literature especially, at least the English pockets of it I knew. It is great to love some things like that and stand by them, to be able to pass them on with energy and conviction. What am I talking about? Headmastering. That's what I was. It was good for me, but not for you.

Your mother was headmaster, too, even more so. Her judgment was better, she could take more stress, and she was funnier. Your mother was the greatest talker I have ever known—and that includes some good ones at Cambridge. She was company, Brian. I loved her every minute

I knew her, and I love her still. She would say the same, I think. That is rare, Brian, and that is good. It must have been good for you too. It must have been. I don't want to sadden you, but to reassure you, by saying you were obsessively in her thoughts during her illness.

Guilt is inherent to life. If you are alive—may you live—you are feeling guilty. Do not feel excessively so on our account. We lived richly, and, as I say, loved. We didn't collapse because you wandered away from us. Which is not to say, sonny boy, that you don't owe us a few. As the world reckons, we were pretty nice folks, pretty damned nice parents. You got clothed, held, fed, sent-to, given-to, sat-up-with, nursed, and even cultured by some pretty good people. So while a long ball is not really necessary, your very kindest, truest self would be much appreciated.

We are forever in the stands, kid. Sorry. We love and loved you.

Dad

Val and Frank,

Jenkins has mercifully turned on the gas.
This is not a tragedy. I am used up—Meg in December. You were family and I love you for it.

J.

Mrs. Dorothy Weimer
Editor, *The Wells Quarterly*
Gibbs House Annex
Wells School
Wells, Connecticut

Dear Dottie,

Enclosed is a submission for the Spring number.
I know we don't print poems as a rule, but since there

will be no Headmaster's Letter, maybe you could work it in.

Best to you,

John

A SCHOOLMASTER CONSIDERS SCHOOL

Like the seasons but wordier
History teaching history
A dark road stretching back, back
And I have stepped aside
Just long enough to think about it
And its memory
Is big and drab and urgent
There is something old-fashioned about it
Of oak desks and ink wells
Waxed floors and the cane
Of footsteps along cold stone walks
Hurtful days, stained through
With some pulsing infatuation
Days, just days
Fright of first days, waiting days
Proud days, prize days
A sudden recognition
Of cruelty or some small excellence
Days, dressed for school days
Tom Brown's schooldays
Every school day that ever was
Romeo's, Cicero's
All Hellas at their little lyres
A bright road opening wide to me
Ghost children chanting something
About verbs
They are cheering in waves
Hymns from voices clear and sad

And gone as bells
Hurrying bells, evening bells
School bells banging me back
To school.

———————————————————

ABOUT THE AUTHOR

Richard A. Hawley teaches history and philosophy and is currently director of a boys' college-preparatory school. Born in Chicago, he was educated at Middlebury College, Cambridge University, and Case Western Reserve University, where he completed a Ph.D. in political philosophy. His essays, stories, and poems have appeared in a number of magazines and journals, including the *Atlantic, Commonweal,* the *New York Times,* the *Christian Science Monitor,* and *American Film.* Recent books include a selection of poems, *With Love to My Survivors* (1982), an anthology of school fiction, *Coming Through School* (1982), and a book about youth and drugs, *The Purposes of Pleasure* (1983). Mr. Hawley is married and the father of three daughters. He lives in Chagrin Falls, Ohio.